# Faith at Work

*Three Studies in the Book of James*

## Carol Ruvolo

*A collection of the following books:*
*James on Trials*
*James on Works*
*James on Wisdom*

DEO VOLENTE
PUBLISHING

Carol Ruvolo, *Faith at Work*
©2000 by Carol Ruvolo.
Published by  Deo Volente Publishing
            P.O. Box 4847
            Los Alamos, NM 87544

Printed in the United States of America.

ISBN:  0-9658804-3-5

# Table of Contents

# Table of Contents
## Continued

# Faith at Work
## Studies in the Book of James

## How to Use this Study Series Effectively

---

Two books of the Bible have changed my life immeasurably. Paul's letter to the Romans changed the way I think, and James's letter to the twelve tribes dispersed abroad changed the way I live. The two books are very different but entirely consistent. One is filled with skillfully reasoned theology whereas the other bulges with wise practical counsel, but the theology and the counsel never clash. They both form part of the necessary bedrock of faith that enables us to walk worthy of our high calling in Christ Jesus.

As you work through these studies, remember that you are concentrating on one aspect of faith—faith at work—and that these studies, like every other part of Scripture, must be understood within the whole counsel of God.

You also should keep in mind that your time is a gift from God to be used in wise stewardship to accomplish His purposes. Paul advised the Ephesians to make the most of their time because the days are evil, and his words apply to us as well (Ephesians 5:15–17). As you undertake these studies, knowing the following information will help you follow his advice.

*Know why you are studying.*

The Westminster Shorter Catechism asks the question "What is the chief end of man?" and answers it by saying, "Man's chief end is to glorify God and to enjoy Him forever." (1 Corinthians 10:31; Psalm 73:25–26)[1]

Most of the Christians I know are familiar with that question and answer—even those who have never read the Westminster Confession of Faith or the Catechisms derived from it. Not only are they familiar with the quotation, they like it. They don't argue with it or try to prove it isn't true. Most of them will say they want to live by it. However, most of them don't. The vast majority of Christians I know do not live lives that consistently *glorify God*, and they certainly don't appear to be *enjoying Him forever.*

Why not? If they know they should, and they want to, why don't they? You might be thinking, "Because they're just sinners, that's why!" And that's true—at least it's partially true. They are sinners; however, they are much more than *just* sinners. They are sinners who have been *transformed* by regeneration in Jesus Christ. What they were, they are no longer. Sin no longer is master over them because the Holy Spirit now dwells within them and enables them to obey God. *Every* Christian has the ability to glorify God and enjoy Him forever.

So why don't they? Two reasons come to mind: (1) They know very little of the truth contained in God's Word, and (2) They have never learned how to apply the scriptural truth they do know in everyday life.

***Know what you are studying.***

These studies were written to help Christians learn how to glorify and enjoy God by living out their transformation in Jesus Christ. They reflect this author's commitment to the Bible as the infallible, inerrant, authoritative, and entirely sufficient Word of God to humanity and her belief that Reformed theology is the clearest and most accurate restatement of God's biblical revelation.

If you are new to Bible study or have doubts about the infallibility, inerrancy, authority, or sufficiency of Scripture, you would benefit greatly from a study such as *A Book Like No Other: What's So Special About the Bible.*[2] You cannot effectively live out your transformation in Jesus Christ without understanding the nature and character of God's unique revelation in Scripture. If you are unfamiliar with Reformed Theology, begin your study by reading Appendix B, "What is the Reformed Faith?"

If you have been studying the Bible for any length of time, you probably are aware of three basic kinds of studies. **Topical studies** present biblical principles regarding a particular *topic*, such as salvation, prayer, love, forgiveness, anger or worry, and they encourage you to grow in your faith by stressing *practical application* of those principles. **Exegetical studies** focus on examining specific portions of Scripture (usually a book or a section of a book) verse by verse, and they concentrate on discovering the meaning of the passage under consideration. **Overview studies** step back and survey sweeping vistas, usually in summary form, with the intent of building a dependable framework for exegetical and topical studies.

All three types of studies should be included in a

balanced "Bible study diet" that will be most nourishing for a growing Christian. The studies in the **Faith at Work** series are something of a combination: they examine specific passages of the book of James verse by verse, but they also concentrate on specific topics contained within those verses.

### *Know what to watch out for.*

Exegetical and overview studies are extremely important and nourishing for growing Christians, but they sometimes stop short of *practical application*. Whenever you undertake an exegetical or overview study, be sure you follow through by applying what you have learned to your daily life.

Topical studies are very beneficial because they stimulate believers to grow and mature in their faith; however, they are prone to at least two pitfalls that require alertness on your part: (1) context abuse, and (2) selective proof texting.

*Context abuse* occurs when a verse or passage is isolated from its surroundings to support a point. For example, how many times have you heard Matthew 18:20 ("For where two or three have gathered together in My name, there I am in their midst") or Matthew 18:19 ("Again I say to you, that if two of you agree on earth about anything that they may ask, it shall be done for them by my Father who is in heaven") referenced in teaching about prayer? Actually, those verses were spoken by Jesus in a discussion of what is commonly known as church discipline, not prayer. Many erroneous doctrines about prayer, however, have been built on this abuse of context.

*Selective proof texting* occurs when only those verses that seem to support a particular view are cited but those that could be used to refute that view are ignored. You may have heard *selective proof texting* in discussions about whether salvation can be lost or forfeited. Those who say a believer can lose his or her salvation may refer to Galatians 5:4, Hebrews 6:4-5, Hebrews 10:26–27, and 2 Peter 3:17 but neglect to mention John 10:27–30 or Romans 8:31–39, whereas those who hold the other view will do just the opposite. It's no wonder people say, "You can prove anything you want from the Bible."

Topical studies require you to follow the example of the noble Bereans in Acts 17 by "examining the Scriptures daily, to see whether these things [are] so" (v. 11). Even if you are new to Bible study, you can follow the example of these noble Bereans by developing the habit of (1) always checking the context of isolated verses, and (2) identifying what else the Bible says about the subject you are studying.

**Check the context.** The Bible originally was not written with chapter and verse designations. Those were added later by translators to make it easier for readers to find specific ideas. Originally, the Bible was written in sentences and paragraphs like any other piece of literature. Remembering this will help you check the context of isolated verses.

Locate the verse in question in your Bible and identify where the *sentence* in which it occurs begins and ends. (Some verses are complete sentences, but most are not.) Now determine where the paragraph containing that sentence begins and ends.[3] Read the entire paragraph to identify the subject being discussed; then ask yourself what the isolated verse says about this subject. If you have time, read the surrounding paragraphs to get an even broader idea of the verse's context. Then go back to the study material and ask yourself if the author used the verse appropriately in relation to its subject matter.

**Identify what else Scripture says on the subject.** There are several ways to do this. Begin by checking the cross-references in your Bible. These will direct you to other verses where the same words or ideas are discussed.

You also may want to invest in and learn how to use an *exhaustive concordance*. These invaluable reference books list every word in the Bible followed by a list of the verses where each word appears. Many of them also contain a numbering system allowing you to identify and define the original Hebrew and Greek words that were translated into English. These concordances usually are fairly expensive, so be sure to get the most for your money by buying the one that corresponds to the particular translation you use for study. If you need help learning how to use your concordance, ask your pastor, an elder, or other helpful, studious Christians.

A topical Bible like *Nave's* also can be very helpful because it lists references by topics, allowing you to access verses that may discuss the same idea in different words.

Of course, the best way to identify what else the Bible has to say on a particular subject is to become very familiar with the Bible as a whole. This is why following a systematic reading program that structures daily readings to get you through the Bible in a definite time period is so important. Most of these take you "through the Bible in a year," but the time period is not all that important. What *is* important is that you are reading the entire Bible on a regular basis so that you begin to become familiar with its overall message. Soon you will find yourself remembering (on your own!) where appropriate cross-references are located. A good Scripture memorization program also helps with this process.

### Know with whom you will study.

Ideally, you should pursue both individual study and group study of the Bible. Studying the Bible individually allows the Holy Spirit to deal with you on a very personal basis, whereas group study allows you to learn from other people's insights. If your time is limited, get involved with a group study, but prepare the material individually ahead of time. This way, one set of study materials can do double-duty.

### Know how to prepare yourself for study.

Bible study is a serious task that requires careful preparation. It never should be undertaken in a haphazard manner. Take the time to prepare yourself physically, mentally, and spiritually so that you can give your best effort to the Lord.

**Physical preparation:** Study when you are well-rested and alert. Establish a time and place that is quiet, free of distractions, and conducive to concentration. Get in the habit of taking notes on what you read, and develop a filing system so that you can find those notes later!

**Mental preparation:** Approach Bible study as you would any task that requires thoughtful effort to do well. Expect it to challenge you and stretch your thinking. Expect it to be difficult at times. And expect it to be extremely rewarding! Spend some time thinking about your daily routine; identify activities that should be limited or eliminated to give you the time you will need to pursue Bible study in a responsible manner. Then schedule blocks of time in your day for study. If you think you can study effectively "whenever the mood hits you," you should think again.

**Spiritual preparation:** Always begin your study time in prayer. Ask the Lord to reveal sin in your life that needs to be confessed and cleansed, to help you concentrate on His truths, and to illumine your mind to understand what He has written. End your study with a prayer for opportunities to apply what you have learned and wisdom to recognize those opportunities when they occur.

*Know whose you are.*

Never forget that Bible study equips you *to glorify God and enjoy Him forever.* You glorify God when you live in such a way that those around you can look at you and see an accurate reflection of God's character and nature. You enjoy God when you are fully satisfied and content in His providential ordering of the circumstances of your life. When your life glorifies God and your joy is rooted in His providence, your impact on our fallen world will be tremendous.

I believe John MacArthur expressed these truths very well when he said, "An uncompromising life is characterized by an unashamed boldness that calls us to an uncommon standard. Allow God to do with your life as He pleases, that He might broaden your influence and glorify Himself."

*Know how to approach the study questions.*

Each chapter in this study is followed by three types of questions: **Review Questions, Applying the Word** questions, and **Digging Deeper** questions. The *Review Questions* will help you determine how well you understood the discussion by giving you an opportunity to express its key points in your own words. *Applying the Word* questions encourage you to put your understanding of the chapter's discussion to work in your daily life, and the *Digging Deeper* questions challenge you to pursue further study in certain key areas.

You should be able to find the answers to the *Review Questions* in the chapter's discussion itself, but please resist the temptation to copy words or phrases out of the chapter when you answer these questions. Work at putting these ideas into your own words. When you can do this, you know you have understood what you have read. It might help to ask yourself, "How would I explain this idea to someone else if I didn't have the book with me?"

You should answer at least one of the *Applying the Word* questions. If you do not have time to answer all of them, pray over them and ask the Lord to show you which one(s) *He* wants you to work on. Remember that you are applying what you learned in the chapter to your daily life, so these applications should take some time and thought—and they should be very specific. Avoid vague generalities.

An example illustrating the difference between vague generalities and specific applications might be helpful here. If you were applying the truths found in Philippians 2:3–4 about regarding others as more important than yourself by looking out for their interests, a vague generality would be: "I need to be more helpful and kind to those around me." A specific application would be: "I will call my daughter (who lives in a sorority house on the local college campus) this morning and cheerfully offer to type her term paper while she studies for her final exams. If she accepts my offer, I will do my Saturday chores on Friday instead, leaving Saturday free to help her." Do you see the difference? A specific application answers these questions:

Who?    My daughter

What?   Call and volunteer to type her paper; rearrange my chores

When?   Call this morning; type the paper Saturday; do the chores on Friday

Where?  Call from my living room; type the paper at home on my computer or in her room on her computer, whichever is more convenient for her

How?    Cheerfully

A vague generality does not answer these questions. You can make applications in the areas of your thinking, your attitudes, and your behavior. Just remember to be specific! Vague generalities do not help you grow in your faith and do not glorify God. (See Lesson 6 of the *Light for Your Path* study *Turning on the Light* for more information about application.[4])

*Digging Deeper* questions usually require a significant amount of time and effort to complete. They were designed to provide a challenge for mature Christians who are eager for more advanced study. However, even if you are a new Christian who has done very little Bible study, read these questions and think about them. It will be good for you to be aware of some of these issues so that you can be alert to material you may come across that relates to them.

Remember that you grow by stretching beyond where you are right now, so if one or two of these questions intrigue you, spend some time working on them. And do not hesitate to ask for help from your pastor, elders, or mature Christian friends.

As you work through this study, resist the temptation to compete with other Christians in your group. The purpose of this study is to help you grow in your faith by learning and applying God's truth in your daily life—not to fill up a study book with brilliantly worded answers. If you learn and apply *one element* of God's truth in each chapter, you are consistently moving beyond where you were when you began. Your goal is growth that glorifies God, not impressiveness that glorifies you. Don't ever forget that.

---

[1] *The Shorter Catechism with Scripture Proofs* (Carlisle, Penn.: The Banner of Truth Trust), nd. 1.

[2] Carol J. Ruvolo, *A Book Like No Other: What's So Special About the Bible* (Phillipsburg, N.J.: P & R Publishing Co., 1998). Any of the following resources also will help you resolve these issues:

> James M. Boice, *Standing On the Rock*. Grand Rapids: Baker Books, 1994.

> John MacArthur, Jr., *How to Get the Most from God's Word*. Dallas: Word Publishing, 1997.

Josh McDowell, *Evidence That Demands a Verdict*. San Bernardino, Calif.: Here's Life Publishers, Inc., 1972, 1979.

B. B. Warfield, *The Inspiration and Authority of the Bible*. Phillipsburg, N.J.: Presbyterian and Reformed Publishing Co., 1948.

[3] Some Bibles are formatted in paragraphs; others use bold type or a figure such as this ¶ to mark paragraphs. Check the introductory material in your Bible to determine how to identify paragraphs.

[4] Carol J. Ruvolo, *Turning on the Light: Discovering the Riches of God's Word* (Phillipsburg, N.J.: P & R Publishing, 1998).

# James on Trials

*How Faith Matures in the Storms of Life*

James 1:2 - 25

## Carol Ruvolo

> *"A saving faith is a living and active faith;*
> *it proves that it is alive by what it does.*
> *The reality of a living faith is*
> *demonstrated by its reaction under*
> *adversity."*
>
>
>
> D. Edmond Hiebert

*Faith at Work*
*Studies in the Book of James*

# Volume I

*For Patti,*

*who loves the book of James.*

*When we allow the troubles of the world to interfere with living out a confident faith in God's absolute sovereignty over every circumstance of life, we rob Him of the glory He deserves and deny ourselves the contentment He wants us to experience in our relationship with Him."*

# Chapter One

## *Trouble, Trouble, Everywhere*

---

*Susan sighed heavily as she dropped the morning newspaper back on her desk and fought off the familiar temptation to cancel her subscription. After a week of discipling women who were struggling with everything from unfaithful husbands and rebellious children to terminal diseases and crippling car accidents, she instinctively recoiled from the graphic reminders of the "wages of sin" so carefully and objectively detailed on the pages of the* Daily Journal.*"Oh Lord," she groaned, burying her face in her hands. "How do we deal with all this trouble..."*

All of us can identify with Susan. Every time we turn on the evening news, glance at the front page of our daily newspaper, or chat over coffee with friends, we are reminded of the Bible's affirmation that "Man is born for trouble, as sparks fly upward." (Job 5:7)

Trials, difficulties, and suffering are an inevitable part of life, and Christians aren't immune from any of them. Jesus said, "In the world you have tribulation." (John 16:33). Peter told his readers not to be surprised at the fiery ordeal among them (1 Peter 4:12). And Paul assured Timothy that he could expect persecution as a normal part of the Christian life (2 Timothy 3:12).

It is very easy to allow all the trouble in the world to permeate our thinking, shape our attitudes and control our behavior. Frightening images of potential disaster lurk in our minds as we grow increasingly apprehensive and frantically try to learn more effective ways to protect ourselves. Preventing, avoiding, or surviving an incalculable number of possible harms becomes our chief focus in life. Is this the way Jesus Christ wants His followers to live? Of course it isn't.

Jesus Christ does not want us to live this way for two very important reasons: (1) It doesn't glorify God, and (2) It doesn't benefit us. Glorifying God amounts to living in a way that accurately reflects His character and nature to those around us. When our lives glorify God, they constantly put His attributes on display for all to see.

When we allow the trouble in the world to consume us and control us, we do not glorify God because we conceal the most basic element of God's nature—His sovereignty—behind a wall of fear and unbelief. Our lives lie about God by depicting Him as One who really isn't powerful enough or caring enough to triumph over evil and work all things together for our good.

Several years ago, a popular book concluded that bad things happen to good people because even though God would really like to help us, He just can't. That picture of God is not only categorically false, it is absolutely terrifying. If God is not big enough and strong enough to control evil within the boundaries He sets for it, why should we have any confidence in Him at all?  Is He even God? By definition, no, He is not.

Fixing our attention on the trouble in the world also fails to benefit us. It denies God's promises that His plans for us are for our welfare to give us a future and a hope (Jeremiah 29:11), and that He will not allow anything unbearable to come into our lives (1 Corinthians 10:13). It clogs the channels of free-flowing joy and hinders the performance of life-fulfilling service.

When we allow the troubles of the world to interfere with living out a confident faith in God's absolute sovereignty over every circumstance in life, we rob Him of the glory He deserves and deny ourselves the contentment He wants us to experience in our relationship with Him.

The way we respond to trials tells us a great deal about our faith. All genuine believers in Jesus Christ have abundant resources *in their faith* to face and overcome any trial they may encounter in this life (2 Corinthians 9:8; Philippians 4:19; 2 Peter 1:3-4). Unfortunately, merely possessing such resources does not guarantee that believers will use them effectively when faced with life's difficulties.

Several years ago, I was flying home from a wedding in Los Angeles when one of the airplane's engines blew out. A sudden, terrifying, metallic *twaang* brought the beverage service to an abrupt halt, while several passengers on the right side of the aircraft actually ducked as oil sprayed across their windows. I immediately panicked and thoroughly embarrassed my fifteen-year-old daughter who was sitting next to me. (Fifteen-year olds are easily embarrassed by their parents, but in this case her embarrassment was legitimate!) Since then I have gone to great lengths to avoid flying in airplanes.

Only recently have I come to grips with the full import of my behavior. My panic in the midst of a frightening situation may have been "understandable," but it certainly didn't honor the God I serve nor did it validate what I had been teaching about Him for years.

By allowing fear to overrule everything I knew to be true about God, I failed to glorify Him and missed a golden opportunity to minister to those around me who were frightened with very good reason because they were not prepared to die. I also failed to be an example of living faith that my daugher could follow.

My avoidance of airplanes has done nothing but compound the problem. It tells those around me that my fear of flying is greater than my faith in God. I have tried to tell myself that there is nothing wrong with preferring one means of travel over another, but in my heart, I know my refusal to fly has very little to do with preference. Rather, it has a great deal to do with the extent of my willingness to live in accordance with what I say I believe.

My response to this trial has taught me a lot about faith. It's taught me that it's easier to talk about faith than it is to live it, and that it's easier to teach about faith in a classroom than it is to learn about it from personal experience. It has also taught me that I would rather be safe than honor God. Basically, it has taught me a great deal about the degree of my own depravity and the magnitude of God's grace.

Even though I have consistently failed to glorify Him in this area of my life for several years, He has patiently dealt with me until I am now ready to repent, confess this sin and turn from it. Today I purchased an airline ticket, and in a little less than two months I will use it to visit my mother.

Facing my fear of flying may seem like a relatively insignificant "trial" in a world filled with horrible misery and suffering, but its significance increases exponentially when you understand that it came as a definitive answer to one of my own prayers. As I have grown in my faith, I have repeatedly asked God to prepare me for useful service in His Kingdom. I now understand that part of that preparation is learning to trust Him in all situations—no matter how uncomfortable, discouraging or frightening they may be.

Trusting God involves learning the truth about who He is and how He operates as well as putting that knowledge into practice in daily life. If I want to be entrusted with great things, I must learn to trust Him in the small things. For me, getting on an airplane is a small thing that has become a major obstacle to my continued growth as an effective Christian. That obstacle must be cleared before I can move on.

When God blessed me with saving faith in Jesus Christ, He equipped me to handle *any* situation of life in a way that would glorify Him while benefiting me. *However*, simply possessing that ability did not guarantee results. In order to become proficient at living by faith, I have to practice what I know. The more I practice, the more natural it becomes.

Responding to difficult circumstances in a manner that glorifies God is part of what the Bible calls *maturity in Christ*. God wants His children to become mature because their maturity glorifies Him as it benefits them; therefore, He is faithful to give us opportunities to mature by practicing our faith. Most of these opportunities come in the form of trials, difficulties, and suffering.

Since we humans have a built-in aversion to suffering, we frequently wonder why our all-powerful and all-knowing God couldn't have come up with some other way to help us grow. Volumes have been written in an attempt to explain *why* a good God allows His people to suffer, and many of them make for fascinating reading, especially for those with a philosophical mind set. But when all the words have been said, read, written and digested, the basic answer is always the same: A faithful Christian's response to suffering is something the world cannot duplicate and for which it has no legitimate substitute. As such, it is a tremendous testimony of both the existence and perfection of God. When professing Christians fail to respond faithfully to suffering, their lives tell lies about God.

So, the way we face trials tells us something very important about our faith—how mature it really is. A Christian with immature faith will avoid trials and seek to escape them at all costs, while a more mature Christian will tend to see them as opportunities to trust God as the means of his own growth and God's glory.

Responding to trials with mature faith doesn't happen automatically, nor does it occur overnight. It's an acquired response that becomes habitual only as we study God's Word and take advantage of the opportunities God gives us to practice what we have learned in the power of the Holy Spirit.

## Review Questions

1. What does the Bible teach about trials, difficulties, and suffering in the Christian life? (Include Scripture references.)

2. Explain what it means "to glorify God."

3. How does the way a Christian responds to trials determine how effectively he or she will glorify God?

4. What does the way a Christian responds to trials indicate about his or her faith?

5. Why does God want us to become mature in our faith?

6. Why does God permit (or require) us to suffer?

## Applying the Word

1. Describe a trial you have faced at some point in your Christian life.

2. How did you respond to this trial?

3. Did your response glorify God? How or how not?

4. Did your response benefit you spiritually? Explain.

_____

5. Do you need to repent, confess, and turn from any sin associated with your response to this trial? If so, confide in a mature Christian friend or relative who will encourage you and hold you accountable to follow through with the action you need to take.

## Digging Deeper

1. Read and study 2 Corinthians 11:16-12:10. What kind of difficulties, trials, and suffering did Paul endure during his life? How did he respond to them? Did his response glorify God? Explain. Did his response benefit him? Explain.

2. Have you had to endure difficulties and trials like those Paul went through? How can his example encourage you in your struggles?

*"James is not appealing to our emotions here but to our minds. He is not telling us how we should **feel** about trials, but what we should **think** about them."*

# Chapter Two

# What are You so Happy About?

---

*Consider it all joy, my brethren, when you encounter various trials, knowing that the testing of your faith produces endurance. And let endurance have its perfect result, that you may be perfect and complete, lacking in nothing. (James 1:2-4)*

A friend of mine is fond of saying, "Keep smiling. It makes people wonder what you've been up to." The slightly humorous cynicism lurking behind that statement is, unfortunately, all too characteristic of our society these days. We wonder about people who are happy all the time. We figure they *must* be up to something or completely out of touch with reality.

When we look at the world around us, we don't see a lot to be happy about. Perhaps that's why the opening words of the book of James are so shocking to the modern reader, but probably no more so than they were to his original audience. Contrary to what some may think, the world hasn't changed all that much in two thousand years.

First century Christians didn't have a great deal to be happy about either. The difficulties faced by first and twentieth century Christians (and all those in between) may be vastly different in content, but they are very similar in effect. Life in a fallen world has always made the "pursuit of happiness" a very elusive venture.

A careful reading of James's opening words in verse 2 indicates that he is not being at all sarcastic or cynical when he says, *"Consider it all joy...*when you encounter various trials."

The word *consider* has to do with a mental attitude adopted after due deliberation. James is not appealing to our emotions here but to our minds. He is not telling us how we should *feel* about trials, but what we should *think* about them.

The words "feel" and "think" are used synonymously by most people today, which is indeed unfortunate because the two words do not mean the same thing. "Feeling" is an emotional process, while "thinking" is a mental one. If you are home alone on a dark, stormy night and hear someone breaking in through the back door, you will *feel* fear—but you will *think* about calling 911.

This distinction is important because mental processes are behaviors subject to willful control whereas feelings are not. If I wait for my *feelings* to change, chances are I will never get on that airplane to visit my mother. It's going to take my willful mental determination to obey the Lord, in spite of my feelings, to get me off the ground!

Christians should concern themselves with what they can control—their thinking—knowing that godly thinking develops godly attitudes which will, in turn, affect their emotional responses.

An attitude is a general mental perspective that colors the way we look at life. Optimism, pessimism, humility, and arrogance can all be regarded as attitudes that develop as a result of habitual patterns of thinking. The joy James refers to in verse 2 can be described as an attitude that develops in response to habitually thinking about trials with a godly perspective.

This attitude of joy bears very little resemblance to what the world calls happiness. The Christian's attitude of joy is rooted in the peace that results from knowing we are in the sovereign care of the all-powerful God of the Universe who works all things together for our good (Romans 8:28; Hebrews 13:5).

What the world calls happiness on the other hand, is inexorably tied to people, circumstances and possessions. Worldly happiness slips from my grasp when people act up, circumstances go awry, and possessions disappear, but an attitude of joy endures through all of these things because God never changes.

We can *consider* our trials *all joy* by focusing our minds on what James tells us about them. They are an indispensable part of our growth as Christians. Trials require us to exercise our faith, producing within us the quality of endurance. Endurance eventually brings us to the point of being "perfect and complete, lacking in nothing," a beautiful description of maturity in Christ. When we discipline our minds to focus on the beneficial results of trials, we can learn to face them with an attitude of joy even when we don't feel happy about our circumstances.

Since attitudes grow out of godly thought patterns, a Christian's attitudes should be firmly grounded in Scripture. God designed our minds to lead and control our emotions (Proverbs 22:17-18; Isaiah 26:3; Romans 8:6-7; 12:1-2; 2 Corinthians 11:3; Philippians 2:2; 4:8-9; Colossians 3:2; 1 Peter 1:13). When we allow our emotions to overrule our minds in responding to a trial, we will inevitably miss God's intended purpose for the trial. Without trials, our faith would remain weak and untested, and we would not develop the maturity necessary for effective service in God's kingdom.

Strengthening our faith by exercising it in response to trials is an essential part of the process Scripture calls *sanctification*. Our salvation in Jesus Christ includes three primary aspects: justification, sanctification, and glorification. Justification is a legal transaction whereby God declares us righteous on the basis of Christ's perfect life and atoning sacrifice on the cross. This imputed righteousness allows us to stand in God's presence on the merits of Christ rather than our own.

Glorification occurs when we are translated from this fallen world to the perfect world of heaven. The pollution of sin will be removed from us permanently and our actual righteousness will equal our imputed righteousness.

Sanctification is what happens in between. Obviously God does not save us and take us immediately to heaven. He leaves us here in a fallen world to reflect His glory as we do the work He prepared for us before the world began. Responding to trials in faithful dependence on Him is part of that work, and displays His character dramatically.

When one of my friends was going through a severe trial, she kept saying to me, "This trial would be so much easier to endure if I only knew the reason behind it." Finally, more out of frustration than wisdom, I asked her, "What if the only reason for this trial is to give you a platform on which to display God's sufficiency to enable you to endure it?"

The Greek word for endurance (*hupomeno*) means "to remain under," and is used almost exclusively to refer to enduring difficult circumstances. Endurance is an integral part of the sanctification process because it draws us close to God by strengthening our dependence on Him, sharpening our ability to serve Him, and magnifying our love for Him.

My friend has learned that endurance produces great blessings that may not include elimination of the trial. Her life has become a constant testimony to God's sufficiency in any situation and an encouragement to others who are facing difficulty. I can't help but wonder if those who have endured the most on earth will find the joys of heaven all the more intense because of it.

You may be thinking, "Good for her; she must be some kind of super-saint. The trial I am going through has soured my outlook on life, and I'm not sure I'll ever have a godly attitude toward it. So, what should I do?" You'll be interested to know that her attitude wasn't right at first either, and didn't change until she committed herself to seeking God's wisdom in prayer. That is the subject of Chapter 3.

## Review Questions

1. In your own words, distinguish between the words "feel"
   and "think." Why is this distinction important?

2. What is an attitude? Is it more related to thinking or feeling?
   Explain why James's words "Consider it all joy" describe an
   attitude rather than a feeling.

3. Explain the difference between the attitude of joy described
   in the Bible and what the world calls happiness.

4. Define *endurance*. Why is endurance important in the Christian life? Describe some of the blessings of endurance.

5. List and describe the three primary aspects of salvation. How is endurance related to one of these? Optional: Is it related to the other two? Why or why not?

## Applying the Word

1.  What kinds of things make you happy? List as many of these
    as you can on a piece of paper. On another piece of paper,
    make two columns, one entitled "Worldly Happiness" and
    the other entitled "Biblical Attitude of Joy." Place each item
    on your list in one of these two columns. Which list is longer?
    How would your thinking have to change in order to move
    some of the items from the "Worldly Happiness" column to
    the "Biblical Attitude of Joy" column?

2. Describe a trial you have experienced since you became a Christian. Did you learn endurance from this trial? Why or why not? If you did learn endurance, how did this help you mature in Christ? What specific blessings did you receive from your endurance?

## Digging Deeper

1. Read and study Philippians 4:4-13. Explain why Paul has no problem commanding the Philippians to be joyful. If he considered joy primarily an emotion, do you think he would command them to rejoice? Why or why not? How does Paul connect joy with peace? How does he relate thinking and behavior to joy? Finally, how does joy relate to contentment?

2.  Explain how the man who endured all the suffering described in 2 Corinthians 11:23-29 could have the attitude of joy described in Philippians 4:4-13.

*"... the greatest challenge involved in facing a trial is disciplining our minds to seek wisdom from God when we would rather give in to our emotions."*

# Chapter Three

# *Asking the Right Questions*

---

*But if any of you lacks wisdom, let him ask of God,
who gives to all men generously and without reproach,
and it will be given to him. But let him ask in faith
without any doubting, for the one who doubts is like
the surf of the sea driven and tossed by the wind. For
let not that man expect that he will receive anything
from the Lord, being a double-minded man, unstable
in all his ways. (James 1:5-8)*

Experiencing a trial is never pleasant. Even when
we understand that God uses trials to perfect us for His
service, we don't eagerly anticipate their arrival. If you are
anything like me, you keep hoping God will come up with
some other way to help you grow!

Because trials are, by definition, *unpleasant* experi-
ences, they tend to generate *emotional* responses. Trials are
trials because they make us feel miserable. That is why the
greatest challenge involved in facing a trial is disciplining
our minds to seek wisdom from God when we would rather
give in to our emotions. At times like these, we are frequently
tempted to close our Bibles, stay home from church, and
avoid prayer while we lick our wounds, vent our anger

toward God and wallow in self-pity. If we do turn to God, we tend to seek from Him all the wrong things.

When my father died several years ago, my mother went through a very emotional time. She was recovering from major cancer surgery when my father was hospitalized with suspected phlebitis. Three weeks later, just a few days shy of their forty-eighth wedding anniversary, he died. As if that wasn't enough, she and my father had been struggling at this time with some difficult relational issues with both my sister and me. Like I said, it was a very emotional time.

Shock got her through the funeral, and then the emotional bomb went off. She told me later the hardest part was trying to deal with so many emotions at once. Anger, grief, loneliness, frustration, and fear always seemed to attack in waves, leaving in their wake a huge temptation to sink into self-pity. Fortunately, my mother learned to seek *God's wisdom* for her trial, and responded well to the Lord's blessing on her first feeble efforts to honor Him in the midst of calamity. She learned, as Paul did so many centuries ago, that when we are weak, He is strong.

James tells us, in verses 5-8 of chapter 1, that *considering it all joy when we encounter trials* involves *seeking wisdom in faith* from the Lord and avoiding the perils of *instability and double-mindedness.* When we are drowning in the emotional onslaught of a trial, James tells us to go to God in prayer seeking *wisdom* to deal with the trial—not escape from the trial, not additional resources to deal with the trial, not even a fuller understanding of the trial. God commended Solomon for seeking wisdom when he could have asked for anything (1 Kings 3:5-14; 4:29-30), and He wants us to do the same (Proverbs 23:23; Ephesians 1:17; Colossians 1:9).

Scripture equates wisdom with discernment, understanding, righteousness, and the fear of the Lord (Proverbs 9:10; 10:13,23,31). Therefore, when we seek wisdom to deal with a trial, we are seeking to understand and respond to the trial with a godly perspective. We are asking God to help us see the trial as He sees it and to respond to it in a way that accomplishes His purposes for it. We can take such a self-sacrificing request to God without fear, knowing that He is our generous, loving Father who will not give us more than we can bear (1 Corinthians 10:13) and who sovereignly works all things together for our good (Romans 8:28-29).

My mother felt overwhelmed by the prospects of widowhood. She had never lived alone, and had always depended on my father to take care of things like mowing the lawn, fixing the furnace, and paying the taxes.

He was a true "southern gentleman" who believed women should be protected from the harsh realities of life as they were encouraged to develop their unique womanly virtues. Nearly half a century with this man had left my mother extremely capable in some areas and totally unskilled in others. Facing perhaps a decade or more of life without her "other half" was pretty unnerving.

As she struggled with her trial, she began to see that she was looking at the situation from *her* perspective. She was evaluating her circumstances in light of *her* abilities, *her* shortcomings, *her* fears, and *her* desires. She had a distorted view of the trial because she was looking at it in the light of her own earthly wisdom rather than the pure light of "the wisdom from above." (James 3:17)

Before she could begin to deal with the trial in a manner that would honor God and benefit her, she needed to seek *His will* for her in the situation. As she did that, she needed to avoid the doubt that would lead to double-mindedness and instability.

James reminds us that we have the privilege of praying in faith without doubt. That privilege rests on our standing in Jesus Christ and our confidence in God's revealed attributes. Our standing in Christ guarantees our access to God (John 14:6; Acts 4:12), and our confidence in His attributes assures us that He always does what is right (Psalm 145:17; Hosea 14:9; 1 Peter 2:23).

Doubt reveals one of two things: a lack of assurance regarding our salvation, or a failure to believe that God will do what is right. Doubt prevents us from implementing the very wisdom we need to deal with the trial in a manner that honors God and benefits us. Therefore, before we seek God's wisdom to handle the trial, we must settle our doubts by examining ourselves to see if we are in the faith (2 Corinthians 13:5), and reminding ourselves of the nature and character of our great God. (The book of Isaiah is a good place to start.)

James refers to a man who doubts as double-minded and unstable. James may have coined the term "double-minded," as no other New Testament author uses it, and it is not found in pagan authors before the time of James.[1] It's a very expressive word in the Greek, meaning "a man two-souled." Such a man lives as if he possessed two separate personalities, one that knows and believes God and one that doesn't. He is characteristically unstable in all his ways because he has no solid foundation upon which to stand.

God has no use for him and will not give him wisdom he would be incapable of appropriating.

The fact that we are instructed to seek wisdom, in faith without doubting, does not endorse the popular practice of "taking authority" over a trial by attempting to banish a responsible demon or demand a personally satisfying outcome. Biblical wisdom submits to God's sovereign control over the nature, duration, and outcome of a trial while recognizing that God alone is capable of seeing the circumstances of life from an eternal perspective. We are simply too short-sighted to demand the right to control the course of life's trials.

The faith James is talking about here is saving faith grounded in God's work through Jesus Christ, not faith in our ability to believe in the efficacy of our own words; and the doubting he refers to is doubting God, not doubting ourselves.

---

[1]   D. Edmond Hiebert, *James* (Chicago: Moody Press, 1992), 74.

# Review Questions

1. What is the greatest challenge in facing a trial? Why is this challenge so great?

2. Explain the connection between seeking God's wisdom in the midst of a trial and considering the trial an occasion for joy.

3. How does doubt interfere with seeking wisdom to face a trial?

4. What do John 14:6 and Acts 4:12 teach us about our privilege of coming to God in prayer? (You may have to think about this a bit.)

5. Explain the term "double-minded." Why would a double-minded man be unstable in all his ways?

## Applying the Word

1.  Describe your response to a trial you faced early in your Christian walk. Did your mind or your emotions control your response? Did your response honor God by seeking His wisdom for the trial? If not, what could you have done differently to take advantage of the trial as an opportunity to glorify God and mature in your faith?

2.  Do you know someone who is going through a trial right now? If so, how can you help them understand what you have learned so far in this study? Be as specific as you can.

## Digging Deeper

1. Read carefully Isaiah 40-55, and record everything you find about God's character and nature. How does this "character sketch of God" impact your attitude toward trials?

*"All people, rich or poor alike, must look to the Lord as their sufficiency during times of trial because salvation has a wonderful way of leveling worldly distinctions."*

# Chapter Four

# *Rich Man, Poor Man*

---

*But let the brother of humble circumstances glory in his high position; and let the rich man glory in his humiliation, because like flowering grass he will pass away. For the sun rises with a scorching wind, and withers the grass; and its flower falls off, and the beauty of its appearance is destroyed; so too the rich man in the midst of his pursuits will fade away. (James 1:9-11)*

One of the most intriguing stories in the New Testament concerns a *brother of humble circumstances* and a *rich man*. Onesimus was a humble slave who was owned by Philemon, a rich man who lived in Colossae. Philemon had been led to faith in Jesus Christ by the Apostle Paul and eventually established a church in his spacious Colossian home.

His slave Onesimus, for reasons about which we can only speculate, ran away from Philemon's household, and went to Rome, probably thinking it would be a good place to "disappear." In God's providence, he encountered the

Apostle Paul, who was serving a prison sentence there, and soon became a Christian himself.

Within a short time, Onesimus had endeared himself to Paul by becoming useful to him in the ministry and a comfort to him in his imprisonment. However, Paul knew Onesimus could not stay in Rome. He had to return to Colossae to seek forgiveness from the master he had wronged.

Paul did everything he could to help Onesimus do the right thing. He wrote Philemon a personal letter, exerting all the power of his considerable influence to persuade his old friend to receive Onesimus as a brother instead of as a criminal. He also arranged for Onesimus to travel with Tychicus who had been given the responsibility of delivering Paul's letter to the Colossian believers who met in Philemon's home. By doing these things, he guaranteed a certain measure of safety for Onesimus and expressed his own confidence in the willingness of Onesimus to put his newfound faith into practice. Most of us recognize the story of Onesimus and Philemon as a striking example of the power of forgiveness within the Christian community, but we should also see it as an apt illustration of the truths taught in James 1:9-11.

All people, rich or poor alike, must look to the Lord as their sufficiency during times of trial because salvation has a wonderful way of leveling worldly distinctions. Galatians 3:28 tells us "There is neither Jew nor Greek, there is neither slave nor free man, there is neither male nor female; for you are all one in Christ Jesus," and Colossians 3:11 says, "A renewal in which there is no distinction between Greek and

Jew, circumcised and uncircumcised, barbarian, Scythian, slave and freeman, but Christ is all, and in all."

We live in a prestige-conscious culture that exalts certain human characteristics and conditions and degrades others. The rich, powerful, intelligent, well-educated, beautiful and famous are elevated above the poor, weak, slow, poorly educated, ugly and unknown. Status-seeking, worldly human beings take pride in the things that distinguish them from others and, at least in their own minds, make them a little better than their neighbors.

When a person is transformed through saving faith in Jesus Christ, all that changes. Salvation shifts our focus from self to Christ; therefore, the differences between Christians dissolve in the surpassing value of His glory. We become one in Christ because He is all and in all. Not only does this change the way we relate to one another, it also changes the way we handle trials.

James points out that the nature of the challenges inherent in all trials differ markedly depending on the circumstances of the individual facing the trial. The poor man may be tempted to blame his humble circumstances for the trial or to believe that he cannot deal with the trial effectively because of his lack of resources; while the rich man may be tempted to believe that trials are somehow beneath his dignity and to rely on his riches or influential position to escape the trial. Yielding to either temptation is sin.

It would have been natural for Onesimus to blame all his difficulties in life on his low social standing and to think that he could never overcome those difficulties as long as he remained a slave in Philemon's household. It would have been equally natural for Philemon to see a difficulty such as a runaway slave as an affront to his dignity and to use all the privileges of his high social standing and wealth to deal with the situation.

Both men would have been sinning if they had allowed their worldly circumstances to dictate their response to the trial. A poor man, like Onesimus, must remember that as a believer in Jesus Christ he has been united and exalted with Christ. His low position in this world does not hinder his being seated in the heavenlies with Christ Jesus (Ephesians 1). His union with the Lord provides him with unlimited spiritual resources to face and overcome trials in a way that furthers his own maturity in Christ and glorifies God (Philippians 4:19). None of God's children are disadvantaged.

The poor man's difficulties are not the result of his humble circumstances; they are the result of God's sovereign design. The poor man is not ill-equipped to overcome the trial; he has access to His Father's heavenly provision. God has promised Him everything—in abundance—to do the work he has been called to do (2 Corinthians 9:8). If he finds himself short of resources, he can be assured he is either under God's discipline for sin in his life, or he is trying to do work that God has not called him to do (Hebrews 12:5-11; James 4:13-16).

A rich man, like Philemon, must remember that he came to Christ in humility. Nothing concerning his worldly situation encouraged, enticed, or compelled God to save him; his salvation came entirely through God's gracious, effectual call. Just as his worldly position and wealth could not save him, neither does it exempt him from trials. The rich Christian must face and overcome difficulties in life for the same reason the poor Christian does—to grow in maturity and to glorify God. Worldly riches provide no advantage; the only truly beneficial resources are those stored up in heaven (Matthew 6:19-21).

Worldly wealth is not evil in itself. Many of God's faithful saints down through the ages have been rich in the world's goods. God is not nearly as concerned about the bottom line of our personal balance sheets as He is about our attitude toward Him.

Do we recognize that all we have, whether a little or a lot, comes from Him, and that it has been entrusted to us to use for His purposes, not our own? Do our daily lives reflect contentment, regardless of our circumstances? Are we willing to move between want and plenty, hardship and comfort at God's call without complaint? Are we willing to give up (or accept) any possession, privilege, or position to further God's kingdom? Are we willing to minister to anyone who has a need, and to receive ministry from anyone when we have a need? In other words, have we submitted our worldly situation completely to His control?

James understands that this kind of surrender is more difficult for a rich man like Philemon than it is for a poor man like Onesimus. The humility (indeed, the humiliation!) required to submit to God in salvation is far easier for one who has already learned humility from his worldly condition.

James's comments in verses 10-11 are reminiscent of his Savior's earlier statements to His disciples: "It is easier for a camel to go through the eye of a needle, than for a rich man to enter the kingdom of God." (Matthew 19:24). But we must not forget that Jesus also reminded them, "With men this is impossible, but with God all things are possible." (v. 26). Rich men can be saved and used mightily by God to accomplish His purposes, but in order to do so, they must remember that they are as transient as flowering grass and will one day fade away in the midst of their pursuits.

The poor brother and the rich brother must join hands in a common bond of submission to Christ, and face trials with the common goal of glorifying God by growing toward spiritual maturity, knowing that their perseverance will grant them the same prize— "the crown of life which the Lord has promised to those who love Him."

## Review Questions

1. How might an individual's economic circumstances or social status affect the way he or she faces a trial?

2. Relate the story of Philemon and Onesimus to Galatians 3:28 and Colossians 3:11.

3. What does a poor man like Onesimus need to remember when he is facing a trial?

4. What does a rich man like Philemon need to remember when he is facing a trial?

5. Why does it seem more difficult for the rich to come to salvation than for the poor to do so?

## Applying the Word

1. Read Philippians 4:10-19 and evaluate your contentment level in the light of Paul's words. Can you honestly say that you are content in every circumstance of life? Write down specific examples of discontentment in your life. What does your discontentment tell you about your view of God's sovereignty over the circumstances of your life?

2.  Do you consider yourself rich or poor? Describe a time when your financial situation affected the way you responded to a trial. Did your response to the trial glorify God? If so, how? Did your response encourage you to exercise your faith in Christ? If so, how? If you were facing this same trial today, would you do anything differently? If so, what?

## Digging Deeper

1. Study James 2:1-13 and 4:1-5,11. Use a concordance to look up and study other passages about wealth and answer the following questions.

   a. Is it sinful to be rich? Explain.

   b. Is financial wealth a sign of God's favor? Explain.

c. What particular temptations to sin do the rich face that the poor do not?

d. What opportunities for service do the rich enjoy that the poor do not?

e. Do you believe it is easier for a rich man or a poor man to live a life that honors God? Explain.

f. If you are not already, would you like to be rich? Why or why not?

*"Perseverance through trials verifies the existence of God's love residing in us; thus, perseverance is the mark of a true saint..."*

# Chapter Five

# The Crown of Life

---

*Blessed is a man who perseveres under trial; for once he has been approved, he will receive the crown of life, which the Lord has promised to those who love Him. (James 1:12)*

The story is told of a small southern town located in the heart of the Bible Belt that was home to two lively churches—one of the Baptist and one of the Methodist persuasion. These two churches had built impressive new buildings right next door to each other on the main street of town and seemed to thrive on friendly (and sometimes not so friendly) competition.

One Sunday morning in mid-June when all the windows in the new buildings were open wide for the enjoyment of the scrubbed and shiny congregations, the Baptist song leader rose to his feet and led his people in a stirring rendition of a popular old hymn, "Will there Be any Stars in My Crown?". Confident that the powerful singing of his congregation had "one-upped" the Methodist song leader next door, he sat down with a satisfied smile that quickly faded.

The Methodists had apparently been so impressed with the Baptists' musical query that they were moved to respond. Through the two sets of open windows the Baptist congregation could clearly hear the Methodists belting out the equally popular old hymn, "No, Not One!"

I have always found that story amusing—not only because it points out the silliness of much of the competition that goes on among Christians, but also because it illustrates the lack of biblical content in many of our popular hymns.

The Bible doesn't teach that our rewards in heaven will consist of a number of stars in a crown. Instead, it describes a number of different crowns that will be received by believers who have performed different types of service for God. One of those crowns is described here in James 1:12. Those who persevere under trials can look forward to receiving the *crown of life* which the Lord has promised to those who love Him.

Perseverance under trial is a measure of our love for the Lord—not the world's emotion-laden love, but the self-sacrificial *agape* described in 1 Corinthians 13:4-8a. We can love God in this way only when we have been so loved by Him first (1 John 4:19). *Agape* is not natural to human beings; its only source is God. Men and women who belong to God are always conduits of *agape*, never its source. God gives us His *agape* and then demands that we give it back to Him by denying ourselves, taking up our crosses (upon which we have crucified self) daily and following Him (Luke 9:23) anywhere He chooses to lead us.

When He leads through difficulties, and fear causes us to stumble, we must take refuge in the strength of His love for us. This is the very love He asks us to return to

Him by trusting His provision and care in all circumstances. Perseverance through trials verifies the existence of God's love residing in us; thus, perseverance is the mark of a true saint, one who will be glorified with Christ.

The words "has been approved" in verse 12 carry the idea of testing for genuineness. We are *approved* by trials just as precious metals are tested by fire. In the refining process tons of ore go into the fire but only the genuine metal survives intact and purified. Likewise, Christians who go through God's refining process burn off ungodliness and worldliness until they stand before Him perfected and completed.

James 1:12 does not promise us that Christians will go through trials without trauma, pain, resistance, agony, distress, or discouragement. Christ's disciples are never promised immunity from the physical or emotional effects of trials, but when they seek God's wisdom (v. 5), they can endure these temporary effects with joy, because they understand the eternal value of the end result—their perfection and completion in Christ.

Those who are approved will receive the crown of life. Because this crown has been reserved for those who love the Lord, I am convinced that all believers will receive this crown. You simply cannot be a Christian without loving the Lord, and you can't love Him without following Him (Matthew 22:37-40; Titus 2:11-14). Not all Christians love and follow with the same consistency or intensity, but they all love and follow.

Being motivated to service in this life by the promise of rewards in heaven should be a manifestation of our love for Christ, not a selfish pursuit. If you have children, I'm sure you have struggled with this issue the same way I have from time to time. Is it right to reward your children (with money, special treats, favorite activities or whatever) for doing chores around the house, getting good grades, and behaving properly? Or by doing that, are you instilling a "what's-in-it-for-me" attitude that works against the qualities of responsibility and unselfishness you want to instill in them? Well, my only child is grown now and I'm still not sure I know the right answers to those questions; however, her response to receiving rewards for service and behavior helped me understand the principle behind the biblical concept of rewards in heaven for faithful believers.

When she was young, we did reward her financially for doing certain chores around the house and for getting good grades in school. By the age of twelve she had become a fairly efficient money manager. As a matter of fact, she had only one major weakness—buying gifts for her family and friends. She would work hard, save her money, and then thoroughly enjoy spending it *all* on other people. I began to wonder if I should try to correct this trait when I suddenly realized she was demonstrating in her life precisely what the Bible teaches about our rewards in heaven!

The book of Revelation contains one vivid description after another of the central activity of heaven, which will be worshipping God and Christ Jesus. Our focus will not be on our own accomplishments in Heaven; it will be on the glory of our Father and our Lord. We will not be parading around heaven, balancing our crowns on our egocentric heads and comparing ourselves to others. We will be using those rewards to honor God and Jesus Christ.

We *should* look forward to receiving rewards in heaven so we will have something to cast at the feet of our Lord. The properly motivated Christian "works for rewards in heaven" in anticipation of the sheer joy of having an abundance to give away in extravagant worship of the Lord to whom we owe everything worthwhile in life. Thus, piling up crowns in heaven becomes not a selfish motivation at all, but the purest and highest motivation of all.

## Review Questions

1. Who will receive the crown of life and for what reason will they receive it?

2. Read 1 Corinthians 13:4-8a and describe the self-sacrificial *agape* love defined there.

3. What do 1 John 4:19 and Luke 9:23 tell us about self-sacrificial *agape* love?

4. Explain what James means when he says that those who persevere under trials will be *approved*.

5. Is looking forward to receiving crowns (rewards) in heaven a selfish desire? Why or why not?

## Applying the Word

1. The following chart contains each characteristic of agape love listed in 1 Corinthians 13:4-8a. In the middle column of this chart list an example of how God's love toward you reflects each of these characteristics. In the right column list an example of how your love toward God and/or other people could display each of these characteristics. Be as specific as you can in your examples. Avoid generalities.

| 1 Corinthians 13:4-8a | God's Love | My Love |
|---|---|---|
| patient | | |
| kind | | |
| not jealous (does not envy) | | |
| does not brag | | |
| is not arrogant | | |
| does not act unbecoming | | |
| does not seek its own(is not self seekng) | | |

| 1 Corinthians 13:4-8a | God's Love | My Love |
|---|---|---|
| is not provoked (is not easily angered) | | |
| does not take into account a wrong suffered | | |
| does not rejoice in unrighteousness | | |
| rejoices in truth | | |
| bears all things | | |
| believes all things | | |
| hopes all things | | |
| endures all things | | |
| never fails | | |

2.  Based on the preceding chart, explain any connections you see between the way God first loved you and the way you should love God and others. Which specific characteristics of love are difficult for you? Which are easy? How can you begin to improve in those areas that are difficult for you?

## Digging Deeper

1. Using a concordance and any other reliable biblical reference books, do a study on "crowns," and then fill in the following chart:

| Name of  crown | Who receives this crown | Reason for receiving this crown |
|---|---|---|
|  |  |  |

Which crowns do you believe you will receive?  Why?

*"A **peirasmos** can be either an opportunity to glorify God by relying on His strength to endure a trying situation and grow toward maturity; or it can be a temptation to sin by allowing ourselves to be enticed and carried away by our own lust."*

# Chapter Six

## This is a Test...This is Only a Test

*Let no one say when he is tempted, "I am being tempted by God"; for God cannot be tempted by evil, and He Himself does not tempt anyone. But each one is tempted when he is carried away and enticed by his own lust. Then when lust has conceived, it gives birth to sin; and when sin is accomplished, it brings forth death. Do not be deceived, my beloved brethren. Every good thing bestowed and every perfect gift is from above, coming down from the Father of lights, with whom there is no variation, or shifting shadow. In the exercise of His will, He brought us forth by the word of truth, so that we might be, as it were, the first fruits among His creatures. (James 1:13-18)*

Since the beginning of time, people have found it easy to blame someone else for their troubles. When God confronted Adam in the Garden of Eden about his sin of disobedience, Adam immediately pointed the finger at his lovely bride, "The woman whom Thou gavest to be with me, she gave me from the tree and I ate." Then when God turned to the woman and asked her to explain herself, she was quick to follow her husband's dubious example by deftly blaming the serpent: "The serpent deceived me and I ate."

Even though Scripture doesn't tell us, I can't help but wonder if Adam and his bride exchanged a sigh of relief (and perhaps a conspiratorial smile) as God proceeded to pronounce a curse on the indicted and convicted serpent. I would love to have seen their faces when He went on to pronounce curses on the two of them as well. I can almost hear them protesting, "But Lord...it wasn't our fault!"

The tendency to blame others for our difficulties reflects the prideful attitude that completely permeates our fallen humanity. Giving in to that temptation on a regular basis is both a mark of spiritual immaturity and a serious sin that God confronts firmly, as the example of Adam and his wife demonstrates.

However, if blaming other people for our problems is a serious sin, blaming God is even more serious. If you read Adam's statement in Genesis 3:12 carefully, you will see a subtle attempt to blame God for his predicament ("...the woman *whom Thou gavest* to be with me..." [emphasis added]). James tells us in vv. 13-15 of chapter one that no one can lay evil at the feet of God, for "God cannot be tempted by evil and He Himself does not tempt anyone." When one of God's sovereignly ordained trials degenerates into a temptation to sin, we have only ourselves to blame.

The word translated "temptation," *peirasmos* in the Greek, has no inherent evil connotation as it does in English. A *peirasmos* can be either an opportunity to glorify God by relying on His strength to endure a trying situation and grow toward maturity; or it can be a temptation to sin by allowing ourselves to be enticed and carried away by our own lust.

Because the Bible is clear about the character of God, we can be sure of one thing—if the trial becomes a temptation, we have only ourselves to blame. God's nature is such that He cannot be tempted by evil, and He Himself does not tempt anyone. Habakkuk 1:13 says in reference to God, "Thine eyes are too pure to approve evil, and Thou canst not look on wickedness with favor." God intends for every trial we encounter to have a beneficial result. When trials result in sin, it is because we choose to heed the call of our human depravity instead of the voice of God.

I am reminded of a story about a slave who worked in the fields of a very cruel master. The cruel master ruled the slave with an iron fist and demanded absolute and complete obedience to his commands. The cruel master was a totally self-centered man who never gave any thought to what was best for the slave.

Imagine the slave's joy when he discovered that the kind and good master who owned the adjoining fields had paid a very high price to buy him away from his cruel master. The kind and good master also demanded absolute and complete obedience from the slave, but he always had the best interests of the slave at heart. Therefore, the slave found it easy to obey his new master out of love and gratitude.

The cruel master hated to see his former slave enjoying his work for the neighbor and would come to the fence between the two fields and command the slave to hop over the fence and perform certain tasks for him. Even though the slave knew he no longer had to obey his former master, he was so accustomed to doing so that he found himself hopping the fence fairly often.

One day as he was working feverishly in his former master's field, feeling guilty and trying to convince himself he really wasn't doing anything wrong, he looked up and saw his new master watching him from the other side of the fence. As their eyes met, the slave was greatly grieved as he remembered that the high price the kind and good master had paid for him was the death of his only son...

That story is not only extremely convicting, it is also an excellent illustration of the truths Paul teaches about salvation in Romans 6. In that chapter Paul explains how our salvation in Jesus Christ breaks the *power* of sin in our lives but leaves our ability to sin intact.

In Romans 6:6 Paul says "that our old self was crucified with Him, that our body of sin might be done away with, that we should no longer be slaves to sin," and in 6:12 he says, "Therefore do not let sin reign in your mortal body that you should obey its lusts." Salvation frees us from sin's bondage so we are, for the first time, able to obey God; however, it does not eliminate our ability to disobey Him. Obedience to God requires us to continually crucify our very real human lusts.

The Christian struggles with sin because his transformed nature's desire to obey God is constantly being challenged by the "lust of the flesh, the lust of the eyes, and the boastful pride of life" (1 John 2:16). Temptation to sin occurs when we allow our minds to dwell on those appealing areas of worldly lust. The longer we look at them, the more appealing they become.

Because I am a small woman who leads a rather sedentary lifestyle, I have to be very careful what I eat if I don't want to become a *large* woman who leads a rather sedentary lifestyle! I have learned not to let my mind dwell on rich, calorie-laden foods. I know from experience that the longer I look at them, the more appealing they become—and the more difficult they are to resist. Whenever I am challenged by tempting treats, I have to discipline my mind to think about something else, or I will soon find I don't fit into my clothes.

The temptation to overeat is just like any other temptation to sin. When we fail to exercise self-control in the power of the Holy Spirit by dwelling on the things of God, we will soon find that lust has conceived and given birth to sin. Dwelling on worldly lusts in our minds is sinful in itself, as are the behaviors that inevitably follow sinful thinking. A young friend of mine used to say, "Your body won't go where your mind hasn't already been." He was right.

The birth of sin brings forth death. Death in the Bible usually signifies some kind of separation. Physical death separates the soul from the body just as spiritual death separates the sinner from God. Unsaved sinners experience judicial separation from God because their unpropitiated[1] sin bars them from His presence. Saved sinners never experience actual separation from God (Romans 8:35-39), but when they fail to confess their sin, the harmony of their familial relationship with Him is disrupted.

There is no remedy for physical death, but spiritual death has been overcome by the resurrection of Jesus Christ. God's judicial forgiveness based on Christ's righteousness imputed to the repentant sinner will restore the judicially separated sinner to Him, just as His ongoing forgiveness of confessing believers restores harmony within the family (1 John 1:9).

Christians must never forget how susceptible they are to temptation. The lure of the world is incredibly strong, and we are most vulnerable when we begin to think we are invincible (1 Corinthians 10:12). The only protection we have against the enticements of sin is the power of the Holy Spirit in us. When we allow our minds to be lured away from the things of God to the things of the world, we are asking for trouble.

Not only are we more likely to sin when we tune in to the world, but we are also more likely to accuse God of tempting us. The world does not understand God's purpose for trials and maligns His goodness by attributing evil intentions to Him. When Christians allow themselves to be deceived by the world's lies, they not only fail to reap the greatest benefit from the trial but also lose a valuable opportunity to glorify God by demonstrating the sufficiency of His power and grace to endure difficulties.

Because God is good, He loves us perfectly. As we learn to understand and trust this aspect of His character, we begin to see trials as one of the good and perfect gifts that come down from the Father of lights with whom there is no variation, or shifting shadow.

God knows each of His children better than they know themselves. He created them, transformed them and gifted them to do specialized work in the building of His Kingdom. He knows exactly what each one of us needs to become all that He wants us to be, and He sovereignly controls every circumstance of our lives to accomplish His purposes for us. Even when an enemy intentionally works to bring evil against us, God will use his evil intent to produce a good result (Genesis 50:20; Romans 8:28-29).

When God is for us, no one can effectively stand against us (Romans 8:31).

Trials help us mature in our faith because they teach us to rely on God's perfect love and power even if we don't understand the purpose behind the trial. When my daughter was very young, she fell against a display rack in a store and suffered a jagged puncture wound in the soft tissue of her side. We cleaned and bandaged the wound immediately, but within a week, it began to show signs of infection.

She was too young to understand why I took her to the doctor and held her down on the examining table while he cleaned and disinfected the wound. All she really understood was I was helping him to hurt her. At that moment she could have been easily persuaded that I didn't love her at all since she was much too young to understand the depth of love it took to hold her on the table. You see, I knew what would happen if I didn't require her to endure a trial she didn't want to endure.

As she has grown and matured, she has developed a greater appreciation for the potential benefits of painful situations and for people who love her enough to "hold her down." It has been very gratifying for me in the past few years to see her begin to learn the value of trials.

We need to remember that God does not enjoy putting us through trials. The truth is He loves us too much to allow us to escape them. He knows the beneficial outcome of endurance and He desires the glorious testimony of our confident trust.

The key to trusting God in the midst of trials is remembering that He sovereignly ordains our circumstances for His glory and for our benefit. When we keep that truth before us, we can begin to understand what James is saying—that everything God ordains, even trials, come to us as good and perfect gifts from the Father who loves us perfectly.

Verse 18 tells us that only as transformed believers in Jesus Christ can we understand these truths. God has "brought us forth by the word of truth," and given us new life in Him. The indwelling Holy Spirit who illumines our understanding of God's truth is able to keep us from deception, as long as we commit ourselves to learning from Him.

James reminds the readers of his day that they were the first fruits—the promise of a rich harvest to come. Twentieth-century believers are part of that promised harvest, and as such we are responsible to draw on the life within us to respond to trials in a way that honors God by establishing a pattern of righteousness in our lives.

---

[1] Propitiation refers to the sacrificial death of Christ on the cross that satisfied God's wrath against sin so He could extend forgiveness to His elect.

## Review Questions

1.  How did Adam and his wife respond when God confronted
    them about their sin? How does their response relate to what
    James says in James 1:13-15?

2.  Explain how a *peirasmos* can be either an opportunity to glorify
    God or a temptation to sin.

3.  What does Romans 6 teach about our struggle with sin?

---

4.  How does 1 John 2:16 describe temptation? Can you give some examples of each type of temptation?

5. Describe the process expressed in James 1:15. Use examples from "real life" to illustrate your description if you can.

6. Explain how trials can be understood to be among the good and perfect gifts coming down from the Father of lights.

## Applying the Word

1. Describe a time in your life when you succumbed to a temptation to sin. On this particular occasion, how were you enticed and carried away by your own lust? How did you respond to the lust of your flesh, the lust of your eyes, and/or the boastful pride of life? What did uncontrolled lust conceive in your heart and mind? Describe the sin that was born from that conception. What kind of death did you experience as a result of your sin? Have you repented and confessed this sin?

2. Write an explanation of the lust-to-death process described in James 1:15 that you could use to teach this concept to a young child. Now write an explanation of the same process that you could use to teach this concept to a teenager.

## Digging Deeper

1. Study Romans 5-8. Feel free to use any good biblical reference books available to you and to consult reputable commentaries. When you have completed your study, write a clear, concise explanation of what Paul means when he says Christians have been "freed from sin." (Romans 6:7)

2. Study the book of Job. Did Job ever fully understand the reasons behind the trials he endured? How did God respond to Job when Job sought the reasons behind his trials? Explain how the trials of Job could be seen as good and perfect gifts coming down from the Father of lights.

*"Peace, contentment and joy in the Christian life result from faithfully pursuing the purpose for which we were created."*

# Chapter Seven

## Time to Get to Work!

---

*This you know, my beloved brethren. But let everyone be quick to hear, slow to speak, and slow to anger; for the anger of man does not achieve the righteousness of God. Therefore putting aside all filthiness and all that remains of wickedness, in humility receive the word implanted, which is able to save your souls. But prove yourselves doers of the word, and not merely hearers who delude themselves. For if anyone is a hearer of the word and not a doer, he is like a man who looks at his natural face in a mirror; for once he has looked at himself and gone away, he has immediately forgotten what kind of person he was. But one who looks intently at the perfect law, the law of liberty, and abides by it, not having become a forgetful hearer, but an effectual doer, this man shall be blessed in what he does. (James 1:19-25)*

One of the most consistent and pervasive themes of the Bible is the call for believers to pursue righteousness in all that they do. (Matthew 6:33; 1 Timothy 6:11; 2 Timothy 2:22; 3:16-17; 1 Peter 2:24; 1 John 2:29; 1 John 3:10) Believers cannot glorify God and enjoy their relationship with Him unless they are seeking to reflect the righteousness that is inherent in the nature of God.

Ephesians 2:10 reminds us that we were created to do good works, and Matthew 5:16 tells us that the good works we do glorify God. John 14:27, 15:11, and 16:33 are representative of the many verses in the Bible that teach us that peace, contentment and joy in the Christian life result from faithfully pursuing the purpose for which we were created.

Unfortunately, pursuing righteousness doesn't come naturally to any of us. (Perhaps that's why Scripture reminds us of it so often!)  Because we retain our proclivity to sin after we are transformed in Jesus Christ, we must *pursue* righteousness in order to obtain it. When we cease to make the effort to develop righteousness, we default to our natural sinful inclinations.

If you have any doubts that your natural inclinations are sinful rather than righteous, consider (honestly now!) how you would respond in certain questionable situations if you were absolutely sure you would never get caught or no one would ever know what you did. Someone has accurately stated that character is what you do when no one is looking.

Perhaps the most difficult time for any of us to pursue righteousness is when we are facing trials. James understands that we are quite likely to become angry during trying times and that *the anger of man does not achieve the righteousness of God*. Avoiding anger in order to pursue righteousness in the midst of a trial involves listening to God, controlling our speech, receiving the word of God implanted, and doing what He says.

Verse 19 says we must be quick to hear, slow to speak and slow to anger. We cannot pursue righteousness in a trial until we are willing to listen carefully to God's truth regarding both the purpose of the trial and the way He wants us to respond to it. Thus, the first step in dealing with a trial is to seek God's wisdom through prayerful study of His Word.

Secondly, we must be slow to speak. Human beings have a compulsive desire to talk about their difficulties—to anyone who will listen for as long as they will listen. We talk to friends, parents, spouses, pastors, store clerks, bartenders. We complain, we fret, we speculate, we threaten, we moan, we "vent." It's interesting that "counseling" is often referred to as *talk-therapy.* How often have you heard, "Oh, he just needed someone to listen to him talk about his problem."? How often have you thanked someone for "just listening"?

James says, "When you have a problem, be *slow to speak.* Don't run all over town talking about your problem. Close your mouth and listen to God."

Being quick to hear and slow to speak is a very difficult assignment for fallen human beings; however, *transformed* fallen human beings can do it. The indwelling Holy Spirit is always ready to help us seek God's wisdom so we can develop a righteous attitude toward the trial and respond to it with righteous behavior. When we remember to lean on His enabling power, we are less likely to become angry about the trial and respond unrighteously.

When we respond to a trial in anger—either against God or against our fellow man, we short-circuit God's intended purpose for the trial. The anger of man does not produce the righteousness of God. When we allow anger to control our response to a trial, we hinder the development of righteousness in our lives, we do not glorify God, and we stifle our own joy.

Accomplishing God's purposes in a trial involves more than closing our mouths and listening to God, however. It also involves *doing* what we hear Him say. God's written word tells us everything we need to know to live in a manner that pleases Him (Psalm 19:7-14; 2 Timothy 3:15-17; 2 Peter 1:3-4). We cannot listen to God if we ignore His written revelation. But, even a thorough knowledge of God's Word will not get us through a trial righteously unless we put that knowledge into practice. This is why James tells us to receive the Word implanted.

God's Word implanted will grow and bear fruit under the right conditions. If you have ever done any gardening, you know that sticking a seed in the ground and covering it with dirt doesn't guarantee growth and fruitfulness. If you want your seed to grow, you must stimulate its growth by watering it, fertilizing it, keeping it in the sun, and perhaps supporting it with stakes or wires. You must also eliminate hindrances to its growth by protecting it from things like pounding hail storms, unexpected frosts, and dastardly predators (such as bugs, worms, and the next door neighbor's dog!)

God's Word implanted in our hearts must be culti-vated in much the same way. We stimulate its growth by establishing routine habits of worship, prayer, study, fellowship, and righteous behavior. We eliminate hindrances to its growth by putting aside all filthiness and all that remains of wickedness, that is, by avoiding and resisting temptation, examining our hearts regularly and confessing all known sin.

Christians in our society are growing increasingly insensitive to sin and its devastating effects on their lives.[1] One of the reasons behind this trend is the Church's infatuation with the self-esteem teachings of modern psychology. As we become more and more focused on esteeming, exalting, satisfying, and fulfilling *ourselves,* we become less focused on glorifying God. As we increase, He decreases.

Our increasing self-centeredness encourages us to justify, excuse, or ignore our sin because recognizing and confessing sin does nothing to enhance our self-image. What we have forgotten in this tragic shift of focus is that sin is an abomination to God, and that the Christian's purpose in life is to glorify God—not exalt himself. We must be more concerned with what sin does to our relationship with God than we are with what acknowledging our sin will do to our pride.

Another unfortunate outcome of the church's growing infatuation with "selfism" is an increasing reluctance to accept and endure trials as an important and necessary element of our maturity in Christ. The Theology of Self-Esteem exalts a "god of love" who wants us to feel good about ourselves and doesn't want us to suffer. Trials and difficulties are presented as devices of the devil sent to destroy our confidence in ourselves and in our "loving god."

The proper Christian response to trials, according to this line of thinking, is to avoid them, escape them or "take authority over them" even if we have to disobey God's written Word to do it. I cringe every time I hear a Christian say something like, "I know what the Bible says about divorce, but I also know God doesn't want me to be this miserable." God's primary concern is our holiness—not our happiness (Titus 2:11-14). As a matter of fact, the only way a true child of God can know full joy in life (which far surpasses human happiness) is to pursue holiness.[2]

Trials play a vital part in developing a holy and righteous lifestyle, and should be considered all joy because of their potential to mature us and glorify God. In order for that potential to be realized, we must listen to God, eliminate known sin from our lives, and then practice doing the Word. James tells us to examine the Scriptures intently, as if we were examining our own faces in a mirror, and then do something about what we see.

I don't know about you, but when I examine my face intently in a mirror, I am usually trying to repair or conceal the ravages of time.  Once I have determined what needs to be done, I must remain in front of the mirror and allow it to guide me while I work to remedy the situation. I can't fix my face by looking away from the mirror to the wall. In the same way, I can't implement godly conduct in a trial by looking away from Scripture to the world. I need to know God's Word and do what it says regardless of what the secular experts say.

When we deal with trials by listening to God and acting on His Word, His purposes will be accomplished, and we will be blessed in all we do. Knowing this, we can certainly consider it all joy when we encounter various trials.

[1] For an excellent analysis of and solution to this problem, see John MacArthur Jr., *The Vanishing Conscience.* Dallas: Word Publishing, 1994.

[2] For more information about pursuing holiness, see Jerry Bridges, *The Pursuit of Holiness.* Colorado Springs: Navpress, 1978.

## Review Questions

1. How does being quick to hear and slow to speak help us respond to trials in a manner that glorifies God?

2. How does being quick to hear and slow to speak inhibit our natural tendency to become angry about trials?

3. How does the Holy Spirit help us listen to God during a trial?

---

4. What kinds of habits encourage the growth of the implanted word in our hearts? What kinds of actions hinder that growth? Explain how these habits encourage and hinder that growth.

5. Explain how exalting self interferes with glorifying God.

6. Explain the mirror analogy James uses in chapter 1, verses 23-25.

## Applying the Word

1. For a period of one month, make a point of seeking God's wisdom through Bible study and prayer *before* you talk to another person about difficulties or trials. If this is a new practice for you, record how this practice changes your attitude and behavior during trials.

2. For a period of one month, keep a record of your responses to trials. Record each trial you face during the month, including the date, time of day, and a description of the circumstances. Also record detailed descriptions of your initial and long-term responses to the trial. At the end of the month, evaluate your responses. Do you typically respond in anger to trials? Do you tend to talk too much about your trials? Do you habitually listen to God during a trial? Do you need to confess any sin associated with your response to these trials? Do you need to repair any relationships with people? What changes do you need to make in the way you respond to trials? How will you go about making these changes?

## Digging Deeper

1. Using a concordance and any other reliable study tools available to you, do a study on biblical commands regarding the call to pursue righteousness in our lives.

2. Based on your study of James 1, explain how the anger of man impacts our response to this call to pursue righteousness in our lives.

*"We should not wait until we are reeling from another of the world's blows to start thinking about how to handle the situation."*

# Chapter Eight

## Be Prepared

---

Not long after we were married, my husband bought a little plaque for me to hang over my desk that read, LORD, GRANT ME PATIENCE... AND I WANT IT RIGHT NOW! I was amazed at how well he had gotten to know me in such a short time. I enjoyed that little plaque until a friend reminded me that patience comes through tribulation (Romans 5:3-5). Then I began to wonder if I should quit praying for patience!

Fortunately, God does not leave decisions like these up to me. Galatians 5:22-23 tells us that patience is one element of the nine-fold fruit of the Spirit, and Romans 8:9 leaves no doubt that all Christians possess the indwelling Holy Spirit. Therefore, as a believer in Jesus Christ, my life will reflect the fruit of that indwelling Spirit to some degree.

Developing that fruit into full flower is a joint effort between God and me. Philippians 2:12-13 says, "So then, my beloved, just as you have always obeyed, not as in my presence only, but now much more in my absence, work out your salvation with fear and trembling; for it is God who is at work in you, both to will and to work for His good pleasure."

God sovereignly ordains the circumstances of my life to make sure I have plenty of opportunities to cultivate and nourish the fruit of the Spirit, and He gives me the Spirit's power to enable me to respond to those circumstances in ways that will accomplish His purposes. My responsibility is to stay alert to those opportunities and make every effort to respond to them righteously.

Among those sovereignly ordained opportunities to develop the fruit of the Spirit (particularly patience) are the trials we encounter in this fallen world. The first chapter of James has given us some valuable guidance regarding our response to trials, but before we leave this subject, we need to consider one final issue—preparing to face trials.

One of the women I know is an attorney who works very hard to prepare her "trial strategy" before she goes into court. She prepares carefully *before* she walks into the courtroom so she will be ready to deal with a wide variety of contingencies. She doesn't wait until she hears the opposing attorney's arguments to begin preparing her case. She doesn't always use everything she has prepared, but she is rarely caught off guard.

We need to prepare for trials the same way she does. We should not wait until we are reeling from another of the world's blows to start thinking about how to handle the situation. We need to prepare ourselves *beforehand*. Another little plaque that hangs over my desk illustrates this principle very well. It looks like this:

**PLAN AHE**
**A**
**D**

That little plaque is instructive as well as amusing because it illustrates so clearly what happens when we fail to heed the advice it gives.

A helpful "trial strategy" for Christians who want to glorify God and enjoy Him forever should include the following elements. Remember, however, that God deals with His children as individuals, so you should consider expanding or adapting this outline to fit your particular situation.

First of all, *expect* to encounter trials in your life. First Peter 4:12 says, "Beloved, do not be surprised at the fiery ordeal among you, which comes upon you for your testing, as though some strange thing were happening to you." Trials are an essential part of Christian maturity, and should not surprise us.

Second, take full advantage of the non-trying times in your life to learn all you can from God's Word about facing trials. I often tell people the best time to give someone a copy of *James on Trials* is not when they are in the midst of struggling with a major calamity. Most of us find it very difficult to concentrate on learning new skills when we are distraught. We also tend to be somewhat less than receptive to those who encourage us to "change our attitudes" when we are physically or emotionally distressed. You will learn God's principles for facing trials much more effectively if you study them *before* you need to put them into practice.

Third, maintain regular habits of Bible study, prayer, and attention to godly preaching and teaching. The more you expose yourself to the truths of God, the better prepared you will be to face the routine demands of living as well as major difficulties.

Fourth, develop a support system. Cultivate deep spiritual friendships and discipling relationships. Cherish people who love you enough to hold you accountable to God's truth and to respond appropriately when you need help. I have a friend I don't see very often because we live in different cities. However, we work at cherishing our relationship because we trust each other. I can call her when I am struggling with a trial and know she will gently remind me of the biblical truths she knows I already know. (I also know she will split the phone bill with me.)

Finally, pray for opportunities to grow in your faith. This is a difficult prayer for most of us because growth can be so very painful; however, praying for these opportunities becomes easier when we heed the words of James and "consider it all joy, my brethren, when you encounter various trials."

# Review Questions

1. Explain what Galatians 5:22-23 and Romans 5:3-5 teach about patience. (Some translations use the word "endurance" instead of patience.)

2. Explain what Paul is teaching in Philippians 2:12-13 in your own words, and indicate how this teaching should affect the way we understand and respond to trials

3.  Why is it important to "plan ahead" to handle trials?

---

4.  List the steps in the "trial strategy" recommended in this chapter. Can you think of any other steps that would be helpful to include in this strategy?

## Applying the Word

1. Describe a specific trial you are facing now or have faced recently. Make a detailed plan for dealing with this trial using the principles you have learned in this study. Share your plan with someone who loves you enough to hold you accountable to God's truths in carrying out your plan.

2. How would you expand or adapt the "trial strategy" recommended in this chapter to make it more useful to you as an individual?

3. What have you learned from this study that will help you mature in your faith so you can glorify God and enjoy your relationship with Him more effectively?

# Digging Deeper

1. Study the subject of patience (endurance, longsuffering, perseverance) in the Bible and write an explanation of why "patience comes through tribulation." Do you think a person can develop the quality of patience without encountering tribulation? Why or why not?

# James on
# Works

*How Faith is Revealed in Pure and Undefiled Religion*

James1:21 - 3:12

## Carol Ruvolo

*"How ignorant…are they*
*of the nature of religion,*
*the nature of man, and the nature of God,*
*who think a life of devotion to God*
*to be a dull, uncomfortable state,*
*when it is so plain and certain*
*that there is neither comfort nor joy*
*to be found in anything else!"*

William Law, in
*A Serious Call to a Devout and Holy Life*

### Faith at Work
### Studies in the Book of James
# Volume II

*For Elaine Cotter*

*a precious friend*
*and a stunning example of faith at work.*

# Introduction

## ☒ You Are Here

---

If you have spent much time wandering around lost in large department stores, as I have, you probably have learned to look for the map. You know, *the map.* It's usually located somewhere near the escalators, and displays the floor plan of the store along with a helpful little ☒ marked YOU ARE HERE. Those maps are life-savers for those of us with a poor sense of direction because they help us get *oriented.*

Orientation is easy to lose in the middle of a large, windowless building crowded with merchandise and crazed shoppers, but it's even easier to lose in the middle of a concentrated Bible study. We tend to get so focused on where we *are* that we lose sight of our goal.

And what *is* our goal? It is nothing less than this: an understanding of Scripture that will equip us to live out our transformation in Jesus Christ in a way that glorifies God and benefits us. So—before we plunge into our study of *James on Works*, let's fix that goal firmly in mind by taking a few minutes to get oriented.

*Orientation* in Bible study involves understanding the importance of *context*.[1] We must not approach James

1:21–3:12 in isolation from the rest of Scripture. This brief passage is a small but essential part of the whole counsel of God, and it must be understood in light of its *divine* purpose before it can help us achieve our goal. The best way to determine its divine purpose is to examine its context. So before we consider the verses themselves, let's look at two questions regarding their context:

- Why are these verses in the epistle of James?

- Why is James in the canon of Scripture?

Of course, the ultimate answer to both questions is that God put them there. The Holy Spirit inspired James to write the very words God wanted us to read. But He didn't do that by zapping James into a mystical trance and taking control of his writing hand. Instead, He worked through a providential ordering of James's circumstances.

James was the leader of the first-century church in Jerusalem when it was dispersed abroad following the persecutions recorded in Acts 8–12. As these scattered Christians began testifying about their faith in various hostile environments, many became frightened and discouraged. James, a responsible leader concerned for their welfare, wrote his epistle to instruct and encourage them in the midst of their difficulties.

The core of his message is a no-nonsense reminder of the *sanctifying* nature of saving faith. He begins with a stunning attention-getter: "Consider it all joy, my brethren, when you encounter various trials." He then proceeds to explain, crisply and cogently, how appropriating the sanctifying nature of saving faith will sustain them in adversity by enabling them to rest in God's sovereign care.

The first study in the **Faith at Work** series, *James on Trials*, focused on this comforting aspect of saving faith.

James, a gifted teacher as well as a responsible leader, begins where his readers are (struggling with trials and temptations) and then attempts to broaden their understanding of the faith that has saved them. In our current study, *James on Works*, he skillfully shifts their focus from faith's usefulness in facing trials to its underlying character. And in our next study, *James on Wisdom*, he will expand his readers' horizons even further by revealing how faith generates the wisdom needed to live sensibly, righteously, and godly in this present age.

Why did God see fit to include James in His written revelation to His people? There are many reasons, of course—the most comprehensive being to enhance our ability to glorify God and enjoy Him forever. If we are to fulfill our two-fold "chief end,"[2] we must understand that faith does more than save. It also testifies. Faith testifies by equipping us to live in a manner that reveals God's nature to a lost and dying world—and by encouraging us while we do so. Lived-out faith is the quintessential means by which transformed sinners glorify God, and it is the very best medicine for doubt and discouragement. God has so designed it that the more it glorifies Him, the more it builds us up. John Piper said it well: "God is most glorified in us when we are most satisfied in Him."[3]

As we work through this study of a short passage in James, remember the lesson of the department store map: The whole purpose of knowing where we are is to help us arrive at our goal. These few powerful verses must be understood in their context and applied in our lives before they will magnify our witness and increase our joy.

May the Lord of Glory, who alone is worthy of our best efforts, bless our minds with right understanding, our hearts with loving gratitude, and our wills with submissive obedience as we undertake this study of His Word.

[1] For more information on the importance of context, see my *Light for Your Path* study entitled *Turning on the Light*. Phillipsburg, N.J.: Presbyterian and Reformed Publishing Company, 1998.

[2] See Question 1 of the Westminster Shorter Catechism.

[3] John Piper, "Man Satisfied in God's Providence," speech delivered at the Grand Rapids Seminar, September, 1995 (Orlando, Fla.: Ligonier Ministries, Tape of the Month, April 1996.)

*Let my religion be more obvious to my conscience,*
*more perceptible to those around.*
*While Jesus is representing me in heaven,*
*may I reflect Him on earth,*
*While He pleads my cause,*
*may I show forth His praise.*

from

*The Valley of Vision:*
*A Collection of Puritan*
*Prayers and Devotions*

# Chapter One

# Gimme That Ol' Time Religion

---

*Therefore, putting aside all filthiness and all that remains of wickedness, in humility receive the word implanted, which is able to save your souls. But prove yourselves doers of the word, and not merely hearers who delude themselves. For if anyone is a hearer of the word and not a doer, he is like a man who looks at his natural face in a mirror; for once he has looked at himself and gone away, he has immediately forgotten what kind of person he was. But one who looks intently at the perfect law, the law of liberty, and abides by it, not having become a forgetful hearer but an effectual doer, this man shall be blessed in what he does. If anyone thinks himself to be religious, and yet does not bridle his tongue but deceives his own heart, this man's religion is worthless. This is pure and undefiled religion in the sight of our God and Father, to visit orphans and widows in their distress, and to keep oneself unstained by the world. (James 1:21–27)*

Good teachers stimulate learning by communicating information clearly, concisely, and understandably. They know how to express complex ideas and processes in simple terms; they know how to stir up enthusiasm for the most mundane topics. _Excellent_ teachers, however, go one step further. They don't stop at transmitting information; they make that information _relevant_ to the lives of their students. They do much more than communicate. They connect.

Clearly, James was an excellent teacher. His vibrant little epistle crackles with practical relevance. It's not a book for armchair theologians and couch-potato Christians. It's a book for doers—for those who are more interested in _living_ the Christian life than merely in knowing about it.

### _Now That I Have Your Attention, . . ._

James connects with afflicted Christians by exhorting them to put their divine resources to work. He tells them, in effect, "Remember, you have everything you need _in your faith_ to live in a manner that will glorify God and bring you joy—even in the midst of trials and temptations. So make use of it!"[1]

James knew their struggles. They needed help, and they needed it quickly. His letter addressed their need. It was not written as a tightly reasoned theological treatise but, rather, as an action-oriented user's manual. It describes faith from a practical standpoint rather than an analytical one. James doesn't wax eloquent about what saving faith _is_; he concentrates, instead, on what it _does_.

The first study in the **Faith at Work** series, _James on Trials_, dealt with James's riveting description of how faith "works" in trials. This second study focuses on the heart of his message: the courage-infusing _evidential assurance_ of true saving faith. The verses that we are studying right now, 1:21–27, are pivotal. They look back to James's introductory discussion of trials while laying the groundwork for his upcoming discussion of assurance. They apply equally well to *James on Trials* and *James on Works* and, therefore, have been included in both.

### New Life

John Blanchard captured the essence of James's message when he said that the experience of the new birth is meant to be followed by the expression of new life.[2] When we "receive the word implanted, which is able to save [our] souls," we receive much more than a "Get Out of Hell Free" card. We also receive "everything pertaining to life and godliness" (2 Peter 1:3). In other words, we receive all that we need to reflect God's attributes to those around us with confidence, along with the responsibility of using what we have been given. And that precious gift comes to us beautifully wrapped up in saving faith. D. Edmond Hiebert describes that faith as "not merely a body of doctrinal truth to which we adhere but rather the wholehearted attitude of a full and unquestioning committal to and dependence upon God, as He has revealed Himself to us in Christ Jesus."[3] In short, the faith that saves us is also the faith that transforms us. It is this joint saving-transforming nature of faith that perfectly fulfills God's eternal purpose for His covenant of redemption.

Have you ever wondered why God saved you? Or why He saved me? Or why He saved anyone at all? Well, He certainly wasn't motivated by anything good or charming or appealing in you—or me—or anyone at all. He did it for His own glory. In Ephesians 1, Paul tells us that God "chose us in Him before the foundation of the world . . . [and] predestined us to adoption as sons through Jesus Christ . . . *to the praise of the glory of His grace. . . .* " He explains that "we have obtained an inheritance, . . . to the end that we who were the first to hope in Christ should be *to the praise of His glory.*" And then he goes on to say that we "were sealed in Him with the Holy Spirit of promise, who is given as a pledge of our inheritance, with a view to the redemption of God's own possession, *to the praise of His glory*" (vv. 5–6, 11–14; italics added for emphasis).

The covenant of redemption—ordained by the Father, ratified by the Son, and sealed by the Spirit—was devised and implemented for the express purpose of praising the glory of God. James knew that, and the Christians who received his letter also knew it. But they weren't *doing* it, and James knew that this was their real problem. They needed reminder, instruction, and encouragement to act out their transformation in Jesus Christ by living in faith *to the praise of God's glory.*

### I Want To . . . But I Don't Know How

If you've done much discipling and counseling with other Christians, I'm sure you've heard more than one person say, "I want to obey God. I want to glorify Him in my life. But I just don't know how." Well, James knew how—and he didn't mind sharing what he knew. "If you really want to live your faith," he says, in effect, "You have to do two things: (1) launch an all-out campaign against sin in your life, and (2) pay very close attention to the law of God." Let's examine his advice.

**Campaigning against sin.** Satan knows he can't undo God's redemptive work in our lives, but he can steal God's glory by polluting our witness. And when we yield to his wiles, we aid and abet his thievery. In order to glorify God, we must be very aware of sin's insidiousness; we must work overtime at "putting aside all filthiness and all that remains of wickedness."

Christians who believe they have sin under control are in the greatest danger from the Enemy. Paul reminds them in 1 Corinthians 10:12, "Therefore let him who thinks he stands take heed lest he fall." If sin doesn't seem to be much of a problem for you, look out: You are standing on the crumbling edge of a very dangerous precipice.

One of the characteristics of Christian maturity is an ever-increasing sensitivity to our own sin. A lady I know who became a Christian in her early seventies told our Bible study group one day, "Before I became a Christian, I never sinned. But now I sin all the time!" Her statement reflects the truth of John Blanchard's statement in his commentary on James: "To the unconverted person sin is generally a trifle, to the carnal Christian it is often a trouble, but to the sensitive saint it is always a tragedy."[4]

If we are serious about living in faith, we must be conscientious in developing and maintaining an acute sensitivity to sin. That always includes devoting a portion of our daily prayer time to asking God to reveal our sinful thoughts, actions, and attitudes. As soon as He answers such prayer (and He will!), we must repent, confess, and ask Him for cleansing and forgiveness in accordance with 1 John 1:9.

Developing and maintaining sensitivity to sin also includes acting decisively to reduce our "natural immunity" to the sin around us. When I moved to Las Vegas, Nevada, immediately following my first marriage, I was shocked by the billboards lining the main street into town. Although tame by today's worldly standards, in 1968 they were blatantly "explicit." Three years later, when we drove out of town to return to Albuquerque, those billboards, which were just as explicit, no longer shocked me. I had built up an immunity to the sin around me. (If you would like to test your own "immunity level" to the sin around you, turn off your television for six months—or even a year—and fill your leisure time with godly activities. Then turn your television on at the end of that time and see how shocked you are at the typical program content.)

Reducing our immunity to sin requires *decreasing* our exposure to sin and *increasing* our exposure to righteousness as much as possible. Paul wisely advises Timothy to "flee from youthful lusts, . . . [and] refuse foolish and ignorant speculations" (2 Timothy 2:22–23). Apply Paul's wisdom to your own life by honestly answering these questions: If Jesus suddenly walked in your front door, would you turn off the television? Would you invite Him to that movie you're planning to see on Saturday night? Do you think He would enjoy the book you've just finished reading? Have you forgotten that you live "in Him" and that He participates in everything you do?

Paul also advises Timothy to "pursue righteousness, faith, love and peace, with those who call on the Lord from a pure heart." Apply this wisdom immediately by replacing unrighteous activities with righteous ones and by cultivating friendships with people who will encourage you to pursue purity and holiness.

**Paying attention to God's law.** Living in faith also requires living in accordance with the law of God. Because God saved us for *the praise of His glory*, our desire to understand and apply God's truths in our lives reflects the presence of saving faith within us. As we act on those desires, in faith, to fulfill the purpose of God's covenant of redemption, we are blessed with assurance, confidence, and joy.

If you're anything like me, however, you often fail to experience those blessings because your practice doesn't always line up with your desires. We can all identify with Paul's lament in Romans 7:18–19: "For I know that nothing good dwells in me, that is, in my flesh; for the wishing is present in me, but the doing of the good is not. For the good that I wish, I do not do; but I practice the very evil that I do not wish."

We fail to glorify and enjoy God when we yield to the attempts of the world, the flesh, and the devil to keep us from looking intently into the perfect law of liberty and doing what it says. God's perfect law of liberty frees us to fulfill His purposes for us and receive His blessing—but only if we work at becoming effectual doers instead of forgetful hearers.

Effectual doers delight in the law of the Lord and meditate on it day and night (Psalm 1:2). They do justice, love kindness, and walk humbly with their God (Micah 6:8). They put on compassion, kindness, gentleness, and patience (Colossians 3:12). They forgive others as God has forgiven them (Ephesians 4:32). They do not forsake assembling together to encourage one another and to stimulate one another to love and good deeds (Hebrews 10:24–25). They speak edifying words and refrain from bitterness, wrath, anger, clamor, and slander (Ephesians 4:29, 31). And they *do* all these things because the word of Christ richly dwells within them in the power of the Holy Spirit (Colossians 3:16; Ephesians 5:18).

They are effectual doers—and Psalm 1 tells us they are blessed. In fact, they are so blessed that they are like "a tree firmly planted by streams of water, which yields its fruit in its season, and its leaf does not wither"—and in whatever they do, they prosper.

### That Ol' Time Religion

When I was in college, our church youth group thoroughly enjoyed what our sponsors called "extemporaneous singing." The song we always had the most fun with was the rollicking spiritual "Gimme That Ol' Time Religion." Singing that song became something of an endurance contest as we made up verse after verse describing people "that ol' time religion" was good for.

It wasn't until years later that I gave any thought to exactly what "that ol' time religion" was and why it was good for all those people. I'm sure that the singers who originated that song had Christianity in mind, even though the word *religion* always has had a much broader meaning. When James uses it in his epistle, he is referring to the *activities* of religion, which can be generated by both faithful and unfaithful motives. A person can go to church regularly, pray beautifully, fast dutifully, give charitably, and even perform signs and wonders, only to hear Jesus say to him "on that day, . . . 'I never knew you; depart from Me, you who practice lawlessness'" (Matthew 7:22–23). How can people who have done all these "good" things be rejected on the grounds of practicing lawlessness? The answer is simple: because their actions have been stimulated by a religion of their own creation rather than the pure and undefiled religion of God's creation.

How can we know which religion is stimulating our good works? James gives us a two-fold test—in essence, he says, "Look at your speech and look at your service." Christian religious conversion is characterized by a changed inner life, marked by self-control and self-sacrifice. Self-control finds its clearest demonstration in the way a person speaks; self-sacrifice, in a person's willingness to serve those who can offer nothing in return. The self-control needed to curb our tongues is rooted in *God-given faith*, whereas self-sacrificial service is rooted in *Christ-centered love*—the two graces that always accompany genuine salvation. That is why James returns to both of these issues again and again in his epistle as he describes faith at work.

### Don't Kid Yourself

Three times in the space of his first twenty-seven verses, James warns his readers against self-deception. He knows how easily we all deceive ourselves—particularly when we attempt to examine ourselves. Because David knew he wasn't objective about himself, he prayed, "Search me, O God, and know my heart; Try me and know my anxious thoughts; And see if there be any hurtful way in me, And lead me in the everlasting way" (Psalm 139:23–24). Because Paul knew his own evaluation of himself was too prejudicial to hold up in court, he told the Corinthians, "I am conscious of nothing against myself, yet I am not by this acquitted; but the one who examines me is the Lord" (1 Corinthians 4:4).

The world encourages our natural affinity for deceiving ourselves by exhorting us to build our self-esteem, to live assertively, and to focus on all the good things we deserve. But James encourages us to "keep [ourselves] unstained by the world." The only way we can be assured of the genuineness of our faith is to look for evidence of God's pure and undefiled religion working in our lives. As we work through the remaining chapters of this study, James will help us do that.

[1]  Chapter Six of *James on Trials* discusses the Greek word *peirasmos*, which can be translated "trial" or "temptation." See that discussion if you wish to review the significance of this word.

[2]  John Blanchard, *Truth for Life: A Devotional Commentary on the Epistle of James* (Durham, England: Evangelical Press, 1986), 72.

[3]  D. Edmond Hiebert, *James* (Chicago: Moody Press, 1979, 1992), 72.

[4]  Blanchard, *Truth for Life*, 84.

# Review Questions

1. Explain James's purpose for writing the epistle we are studying and its importance to the whole counsel of God as revealed in the Bible. (Hint: Be sure to read the Introduction to this study before attempting to answer this question.)

2. Think about John Blanchard's statement that "the experience of the new birth is meant to be followed by the expression of new life." In your own words, explain how Blanchard's statement captures the essence of James's message.

3. How does the joint saving-transforming nature of faith perfectly fulfill God's eternal purpose for His covenant of redemption?

4. Describe James's two-step plan for living out your faith.

5. How can we be sure that our "good works" reflect genuine Christian conversion?

6. Why does James exhort us to keep ourselves unstained by the world?

## Applying the Word

1. Are you a doer of the Word? Find out by listing specific examples of how you do the following things:

   Delight in the law of God:


   Meditate on God's law:


   Demonstrate kindness:


   Demonstrate compassion:


   Demonstrate gentleness:


   Demonstrate patience:


   Forgive as you have been forgiven:


   Assemble with believers for mutual edification:


   Speak so as to encourage others to godliness:


   Refrain from bitterness, wrath, anger, clamor, and slander:

In which of these areas are you doing well? In which are you in most need of improvement?

List several specific ways you can help someone overcome his or her weaknesses in an area in which you are strong.

Make a detailed plan that will help you improve in one or more of your weak areas. Share your plan with someone who loves you enough to hold you accountable for following through with it.

2.  List your favorite television programs and the best movies
    you have seen in the past few months. Then add your favorite
    books to your list. Go back over your list, imagining that
    Jesus is sitting by your side. Revise your list until you are
    comfortable with the idea of Jesus participating in these
    activities with you. What does this exercise reveal to you
    about your sensitivity to sin? How will it impact your future
    use of leisure time?

# Digging Deeper

1. Research the biblical meanings of *faith* and *love*. In your own words, explain why faith and love are described as *graces*. Then write a thorough explanation of the connection between *self-control* and *God-given faith* as well as the connection between *self-sacrificial service* and *Christ-centered love*.

*"Unless there is within us that which is above us,
we shall soon yield to that which is about us."*

∞

Spiros Zodhiates[1]

# Chapter Two

# Real Religion Doesn't Play Favorites

---

*My brethren, do not hold your faith in our glorious Lord Jesus Christ with an attitude of personal favoritism. For if a man comes into your assembly with a gold ring and dressed in fine clothes, and there also comes in a poor man in dirty clothes, and you pay special attention to the one who is wearing the fine clothes, and say, "You sit here in a good place," and you say to the poor man, "You stand over there, or sit down by my footstool," have you not made distinctions among yourselves, and become judges with evil motives? Listen, my beloved brethren: did not God choose the poor of this world to be rich in faith and heirs of the kingdom which He promised to those who love Him? But you have dishonored the poor man. Is it not the rich who oppress you and personally drag you into court? Do they not blaspheme the fair name by which you have been called? (James 2:1–7)*

The Texas House of Representatives once passed a resolution honoring one Albert DeSalvo for "noted activities and unconventional techniques involving population control and applied psychology," which made him "an acknowledged leader in his field." The resolution, introduced by Representative Tom Moore, Jr., of Waco, also praised DeSalvo's "dedicated devotion to his work."

You've never heard of Albert DeSalvo? Perhaps you know him better by his self-proclaimed nickname— "the Boston Strangler." Soon after the bill was passed, Representative Moore revealed his real reason for introducing it: He wanted to demonstrate—as vividly as possible—how thoughtlessly most legislators vote on obscure or special legislation.[2]

Tom Moore, Jr., of Waco, Texas, reminds me a little of James. The Christians to whom James is writing also had been acting thoughtlessly and were in need of a vivid lesson. James, their excellent teacher-leader, resolutely (no pun intended) rose to the occasion. Pure and undefiled religion, he tells them, is displayed in the exercise of *God-given faith* and *Christ-centered love*—both of which are incompatible with the display of *favoritism* running rampant in their assemblies.

### *Favoritism Denies Faith*

John Calvin described faith as "a firm and sure knowledge of the divine favour toward us, founded on the truth of a free promise in Christ, and revealed to our minds, and sealed on our hearts, by the Holy Spirit."[3] His words echo those of the writer to the Hebrews, who said, "now faith is the assurance of things hoped for, the conviction of things not seen" (11:1).

*Firm and sure* knowledge requires a solid foundation of established fact; it cannot stand on the slippery slope of unproven theories or wishful thinking. That's why the Bible equates firm and sure knowledge with "assurance." The Greek word *hupostasis*, translated "assurance" in Hebrews 11:1, means "to stand under" and is used to describe the foundation upon which something rests. And the "things hoped for" in that verse refer to all the promises of God given to us by covenant.

The foundation of our hope—our assurance—our firm and sure knowledge—is the *fact* of God's character revealed in His Word (written and incarnate) through the quickening power of His Holy Spirit. As the Spirit illumines our hearts to understand God's revealed truth about Himself, we begin to rely confidently on the absolute veracity of His promises. The Spirit's work of assurance produces conviction, or commitment, regarding "things not seen." In other words, being *assured* of the certain fulfillment of God's promises affects the way we think and act in everyday life. We may not be able to see the outcome or the purpose of the circumstances we face, but we trust God's promise to control and care for us in every one of them. That assurance enables us to commit ourselves, without reservation, to seeking His righteous purposes in every situation of life.

Assurance and conviction are very closely related, but they are not the same thing. Perhaps the easiest way to distinguish between them is to think of assurance as the fuel that fires commitment. Without assurance, we would find it very difficult—if not impossible—to commit our circumstances into God's providential care. B. B. Warfield captured the relationship between assurance and conviction when he said, "We cannot be said to believe that which we distrust too much to commit ourselves to it."[4]

Favoritism, James tells his readers, denies the existence of faith's assurance and conviction. It tells those around us that we have no confidence in the fulfillment of God's promises nor in His ability to care for us in every circumstance of life. It also hangs the dirty laundry of our insecurity in full view of the world. Currying favor with rich and powerful people transfers our trust from the spiritual to the temporal, robs God of the glory that He alone deserves, and depicts His covenant people (that's us) as fools. The prophet Jeremiah had explained this to God's people centuries before James picked up his pen:

> *My people have changed their glory*
> *For that which does not profit. . . .*
> *They have forsaken Me,*
> *The fountain of living waters,*
> *To hew for themselves cisterns,*
> *Broken cisterns,*
> *That can hold no water. . . .*
> *For My people are foolish,*
> *They know Me not;*
> *They are stupid children,*
> *And they have no understanding.*
> *(Jeremiah 2:11, 13; 4:22)*

Misplaced faith is nothing new. God's prophets warned His people about it—and its results—throughout the pages of the Old Testament. And James echoes their message in his New Testament epistle.

Whenever people who are called by His Name place their confidence in anything besides God, they defame His character and short change themselves. James asks incredulously, "Is it not the rich who oppress you and

personally drag you into court? Do they not blaspheme the
fair name by which you have been called?"

"Think about what you are doing!" he seems to be
saying. "Don't live your testimony mindlessly. The resources
you need to live the Christian life are wrapped up *in your
faith*, not in rich and powerful people."

*Favoritism Denies Love*

Several years ago, one of my more outspoken students
shared a forthright and very insightful comment with our
group. "When I started this Bible study," she said, "I believed
that I *thought* biblically. But now I realize that I don't! I am
constantly amazed at how worldly my thinking is."

The lesson we were studying had to do with love, and
one of the exercises asked us to distinguish the Bible's view
of love from the world's. She wrote an excellent answer in
her notebook: "The world defines 'love' in terms of emotion
while the Bible defines it in terms of activity. That's why
love is commanded in the Bible and fantasized about in the
world." But when she began applying this great scriptural
truth to her own life, she was astonished (and appalled) at
how much she had allowed the world to squeeze her into
its mold. Her confessional comment in class launched a
lively discussion of practical ways to "renew our minds"
and change our behavior in this particular area. One of the
passages we looked at was James 2:1–7.

James, in characteristic fashion, doesn't theorize about
biblical love; he illustrates it. His example demonstrates the
incompatibility of gracious biblical love with preferential
"personal favoritism." Those who have been made new by
God's pure and undefiled religion must refrain from worldly

expressions of preferential "love" while striving to love graciously. Biblical love is a *grace* because it is unmerited. It is not deserved by the one loved; rather, it is extended freely by the one loving. First John 4:7–11 exhorts us to love this way as a reflection of the way God loves us:

> *Beloved, let us love one another, for love is from God; and everyone who loves is born of God and knows God. The one who does not love does not know God, for God is love. By this the love of God was manifested in us, that God has sent His only begotten Son into the world so that we might live through Him. In this is love, not that we loved God, but that He loved us and sent His Son to be the propitiation for our sins. Beloved, if God so loved us, we also ought to love one another.*

James confronts his readers with the worldliness of their love by describing their behavior. Making distinctions among themselves based upon wealth and power is blatantly preferential, and not at all gracious. Their behavior does not reflect the way God has loved them and thus is robbing Him of His glory.

### Favoritism Denies the Essence of the Gospel

Their "attitude of personal favoritism" also is crippling their evangelistic efforts. The essence of the Gospel is the graciousness of God's sovereign choice. He shows no partiality in election (Acts 10:34; Romans 2:11) and never extends salvation on the basis of merit (Ephesians 2:8–9). James reminds his readers of the way God operates: "Did not God choose the poor of this world to be rich in faith and heirs of the kingdom which He promised to those who love Him?"

Even though material poverty is not a prerequisite for salvation, God "has chosen the foolish things of the world to shame the wise, and . . . the weak things of the world to shame the things which are strong" (1 Corinthians 1:27). The Church of Jesus Christ was designed to reflect God's glory most effectively by being comprised of "not many wise according to the flesh, not many mighty, not many noble" (v. 26).

The favoritism displayed by James's readers flew in the face of the truth of the Gospel. It encouraged the rich to think they had an advantage in salvation, in contradistinction to the words of our Lord: "Truly I say to you, it is hard for a rich man to enter the kingdom of heaven. And again I say to you, it is easier for a camel to go through the eye of a needle, than for a rich man to enter the kingdom of God" (Matthew 19:23–24).

Real religion—God's pure and undefiled religion—doesn't play favorites. It can't, because favoritism denies the reality of faith, the reality of love, and the essence of the Gospel. Is it any wonder, then, that when James finds favoritism in the lives of believers, he says, "Stop it!"

---

[1] Quoted in John Blanchard, *Truth for Life: A Devotional Commentary on the Epistle of James* (Durham, England: Evangelical Press, 1986), 28.

[2] Paul Lee Tan, *Encyclopedia of 7700 Illustrations: Signs of the Times* (Rockville, Md.: Assurance Publishers, 1979), 1252–1253.

[3] Quoted in John F. MacArthur Jr., *Faith Works* (Dallas: Word Publishing, 1993), 159.

[4] Benjamin B. Warfield, *Biblical and Theological Studies* (Philadelphia: Presbyterian & Reformed, 1968), 402–403.

## Review Questions

1. Relate John Calvin's description of faith to the one found in Hebrews 11:1.

2. Distinguish between *assurance* and *conviction*. Do you think that a person can have assurance with conviction? How about conviction without assurance? Why or why not?

3.  Explain how favoritism denies faith.

4.  How does the world's idea of love differ from the Bible's?

5. Explain how favoritism denies biblical love.

6. How did the "attitude of personal favoritism" displayed by James's readers also deny the essence of the Gospel and cripple their evangelistic efforts?

## Applying the Word

1. List several specific things you "hope for" in your walk with Christ.

Are the things you listed promises of God to you? Use a concordance, if necessary, to locate and record verses containing God's promises regarding the things you hope for. If you cannot find references validating those things, do you have "firm and sure knowledge" upon which to base your hope? Revise your list, if necessary.

2. List specific elements of your behavior (thoughts, attitudes, or actions) that reflect your conviction (commitment) regarding God's promises to you. How does your behavior in these areas reflect specific attributes of God to the world? How does your behavior benefit you?

---

3. Write your own definition of *love*. Analyze your definition to see if it is more feeling-oriented or action-oriented. To what extent have you allowed the world to influence your attitude toward love? If you need an attitude adjustment in this area, take your concern to the Lord in prayer, asking Him to renew your mind and give you opportunities to practice biblical love.

4. Make a specific plan to practice biblical love during the next several days. Use the following questions to help you plan.

   *Whom* will you love?

   *What* will you do for him or her?

   *Where* and *when* will you carry out this activity?

   *How* will you do it? (This question refers to your attitude rather than your methods.)

   Share your plan with someone who loves you enough to hold you accountable for following through with it.

5. Have you or someone you know used evangelism methods that give the impression that certain types of people have an advantage with God? If so, describe these methods. What do Acts 10:34, Romans 2:11 and Ephesians 2:8-9 tell you about these methods? How would you change these methods to bring them in line with God's revealed truth?

## Digging Deeper

1. John Blanchard quotes Spiros Zodhiates as saying, "Unless there is within us that which is above us, we shall soon yield to that which is about us." Drawing on the practical lessons you have learned from the book of James, expand upon this statement to explain how an "attitude of personal favoritism" is incompatible with God's pure and undefiled religion. Feel free to be creative. Write a poem, short story, or a song if you like. Consider composing a teaching outline to use with children or young people. Ask God how He would have you use the results.

*"Men are free
when they want to do
what they ought to do."*

D. Edmond Hiebert

# Chapter Three

## All in the Family

---

*If, however, you are fulfilling the royal law, according to the Scripture, "You shall love your neighbor as yourself," you are doing well. But if you show partiality, you are committing sin and are convicted by the law as transgressors. For whoever keeps the whole law and yet stumbles in one point, he has become guilty of all. For He who said, "Do not commit adultery," also said, "Do not commit murder." Now if you do not commit adultery, but do commit murder, you have become a transgressor of the law. So speak and so act, as those who are to be judged by the law of liberty. For judgment will be merciless to one who has shown no mercy; mercy triumphs over judgment. (James 2:8–13)*

My mother and I sound a great deal alike on the telephone, and people often mistake one of us for the other. During my high school and college days, friends soon learned to ask, "Carol, is that you?" before saying too much. But one memorable day my youthfully overconfident sweetheart neglected to inquire. Hearing what he was sure was my voice on the line, he quipped, "Hello, hot lips. This is your big sugar daddy."

My mother was a bit startled but managed to respond, "Just a moment, please. You have the wrong hot lips." It's a good thing she liked him so much, or our fledgling romance could have ended right there!

Amazing as it may seem, I was reminded of that then-embarrassing but now-hilarious case of "mistaken identity" by reading through the book of James again this week. Have you ever noticed how much James sounds like his brother Jesus?

Most reputable Bible scholars agree that the little book of James was written by the half-brother of our Lord who, although he did not become a Christian until after the resurrection, obviously had been acquainted with Jesus' teachings long before then. The Gospel of John reveals how familiar Jesus' unbelieving brothers were with His claims in the following account of a disturbing family face-off: "Now the feast of the Jews, the Feast of Booths, was at hand. His brothers therefore said to Him, 'Depart from here, and go into Judea, that Your disciples also may behold Your works which You are doing. For no one does anything in secret, when he himself seeks to be known publicly. If you do these things, show Yourself to the world.' For not even His brothers were believing in Him" (7:2–5).

I'm sure James spent many hours after his conversion grieving over his scornful treatment of Jesus and praying for enablement to communicate clearly the truths he had since come to love. It is patently obvious that God answered his prayers, for James's teaching sounds much like his Brother's.

## *The Royal Law*

At one point in Jesus' ministry, a rich young man asked Him a very important question: "Teacher, what good thing shall I do that I may obtain eternal life?" Jesus' answer sounds very strange to most modern evangelical readers: "If you wish to enter into life, keep the commandments. . . . You shall not commit murder; You shall not commit adultery; You shall not steal; You shall not bear false witness; Honor your father and mother; and You shall love your neighbor as yourself" (Matthew 19:16–19).

The rich young man also seemed puzzled, for he asked, "All these things I have kept; what am I still lacking?" The Savior's next words, however, were even more puzzling: "If you wish to be complete, go and sell your possessions and give to the poor, and you shall have treasure in heaven; and come, follow Me" (vv. 20–21).

What kind of evangelism is that? Had Jesus changed His mind about salvation by grace through faith? Hardly. He was describing its very essence. Saving faith *transforms*; it *regenerates*; it produces *new creations* in Christ. Genuine salvation is *always* evidenced in the activities of life. The rich young man would not have gone away grieved if he had possessed a transformed, regenerated, re-created heart of flesh. His unwillingness to part with his property evidenced the unchanged condition of his heart of stone.

I sometimes wonder if James witnessed that definitive exchange, because in the passage we are considering, he sounds so much like Jesus. His words echo his Brother's as he addresses an anticipated challenge from those he is admonishing.

"James, you've misjudged us," his readers could say. "We're not playing favorites by showing that rich man to a good seat. He is, after all, a bit hard of hearing and troubled by arthritis. We just want to make sure these afflictions don't hinder him from hearing the message."

James acknowledges the difficulty of discerning the presence of pure and undefiled religion solely on the basis of external works. He then charges his readers with the responsibility of examining their hearts.

"If I have truly misjudged you," he seems to be saying, "then you have nothing to worry about. But if you are misjudging yourselves, then you are in very grave danger. If your actions are motivated by a transformed desire to fulfill the *royal law,* you are doing well. But if they are motivated by selfish partiality, you are sinning and stand convicted by the law as transgressors."

What is this "royal law" to which James refers? It is the same law his Brother quoted to the rich young man: "You shall love your neighbor as yourself." James understood what Jesus had said. Pure and undefiled religion always will be evidenced by loving actions toward others. However, *selfish actions devoid of love* evidence nothing more than unregenerate depravity.

### *Definition of a Lawbreaker*

Jesus reduced "the whole Law and the Prophets" to the single word *love* (Matthew 22:37–39). "The Law and the Prophets" was a common way of referring to the majority of the Old Testament, where God's righteous requirements for His people and the consequences of their failure to honor them are described. Those requirements are summarized in the Ten Commandments, given to Moses on Mount Sinai.

When Jesus told the rich young man to "keep the commandments," He more than likely had these Ten in mind. Anyone who kept the Ten Commandments would fulfill God's righteous requirements and obtain eternal life—which is what the young man was seeking. He went away grieving, however, because he had failed to grasp that keeping the commandments is an act of love.

If you "love the Lord your God with all your heart, and with all your soul, and with all your mind," you will put no other gods before Him. You will refrain from idolatry, refuse to blaspheme His name, and keep His Sabbath holy. If you "love your neighbor as yourself," you will honor your parents and abstain from murder, adultery, theft, lying, and covetousness.

In His Sermon on the Mount, Jesus described the kind of love necessary to fulfill God's Law. This kind of love knows that anger is as damning as murder, that broken relationships interfere with worship, that lust is private adultery, that technicalities don't justify lying, and that loving your neighbors doesn't stop with your friends. The *only* kind of love that fulfills God's Law is "perfect, as your heavenly Father is perfect." (See Matthew 5:17–48.)

James's teaching echoes his Brother's as he declares to his readers, "*Any* imperfection of love violates God's Law. And one violation means you're guilty of all" (my paraphrase).

## The Law of Liberty

The implications of James's words are staggering, for violating God's Law damns you to hell.

"Wait just a minute!" I hear some protest. "I'm trusting in Jesus, so I'm not under law. I'm under grace and free to do what I want." If your voice is among those, I beg you to listen. You've misread your Bible and are deceiving yourself. Grace does indeed free us from the *curse* of God's Law, but not from the fact of its absolute *rule.*

James's two descriptions of God's Law in the passage we are studying allude to this truth. In verse 8, he calls it "royal"—an obvious reference to its Author, God our King. Because a perfect divine Sovereign wrote the law, it is not only holy, righteous and good—it also is eternal. God's law reflects His attributes, one of which is immutability. The Law never changes because He never does. When Adam sinned in the Garden of Eden, this holy, righteous, good, and immutable God *necessarily* imposed the curse of His holy, righteous, good, and immutable Law upon Adam and his posterity.

But God also is gracious and merciful, and He promised redemption in the very midst of the curse (Genesis 3:14–19). The Savior He promised would not set aside God's Law; rather, He would fulfill it perfectly and credit His obedience to the account of the elect. He would bear God's wrath for the guilt of their sin and then give them God's Spirit to transform them completely and put them at liberty to obey their God.

Therefore, says James, "So speak and so act, as those who are to be judged by the *law of liberty*." (Emphasis is added to indicate James's second description of God's Law.)

Since our desires and abilities have been transformed by the work of Christ Jesus, our behavior should reflect the God who redeemed us. Notice that James did not say we are to act as those who have been *liberated from the Law*, but as those who are now *free to obey it*.

Those who have known mercy should reflect it to others, just as those who have been forgiven should be quick to forgive. Those in the family bear the family resemblance. As we are conformed to His image, we become more and more like Him. A person wholly unlike Him has never known Him.

The Apostle John taught this same truth: "the one who says he abides in Him ought himself to walk in the same manner as He walked" (1 John 2:6). So did the Apostle Paul when he declared that our resemblance to Christ will provide the basis for our judgment before God "who will render to every man according to his deeds: to those who by perseverance in doing good seek for glory and honor and immortality, eternal life; but to those who are selfishly ambitious and do not obey the truth, but obey unrighteousness, wrath and indignation" (Romans 2:6–8).

If you don't resemble your Savior, you haven't been saved and are under God's curse. But if you know Him, you'll love Him and obey what He says (John 14:15; 1 John 2:3). John Blanchard has said that a person without mercy is a person without love; a person without love is a person without grace; and a person without grace is a person without God.[1] That's why "judgment will be merciless to one who has shown no mercy" and why "mercy triumphs over judgment." Once again James sounds much like his Brother. "Blessed are the merciful," said Jesus in His Sermon on the Mount, "for they shall receive mercy" (Matthew 5:7).

[1] John Blanchard, *Truth for Life: A Devotional Commentary on the Epistle of James* (Durham, England: Evangelical Press, 1986), 157.

# Review Questions

1. Describe the similarities between what Jesus told the rich young man and what James says to his potential challengers.

2. Describe the essence of saving faith and explain what it has to do with the "royal law."

3. Explain how loving God and loving your neighbor fulfills God's law. What kind of love is needed to do this?

4. What does it mean to be under the curse of God's law? Does being free from the Law's curse mean that we are free from its rule? Why or why not? (Hint: Read Matthew 5:17-20 and think about the difference between being liberated from the law and being liberated to obey it.)

5. Why will judgment be merciless to one who has shown no mercy?

6. How does mercy triumph over judgment?

## Applying the Word

1. Look up the words *mercy* and *merciful* in both a standard dictionary and in a Bible or theological dictionary. Then write a definition in your own words.

   *mercy:*

   *merciful:*

   List several specific ways in which God has been merciful to you.

   Now list several specific ways in which you have extended mercy to others. The following questions will help you be specific:

   To whom have you been merciful?

   What did you do that was merciful?

   When and where were you merciful?

How (in reference to your attitude) did you extend mercy?

Based on your answers to the above exercises, prayerfully consider and answer the following questions:
Are you a merciful person?

What does the quality of your mercy reveal about your walk with the Lord?

What changes do you need to make in your life in order to be a more merciful person?

How will you go about making these changes?

2.  List several specific ways in which you could reflect your
    transformation in Jesus Christ by loving your neighbor this
    week. In your answer, be sure to identify your neighbor;
    specify what, when, and where you will love that neighbor;
    and how this action will reflect your transformed nature and
    thereby glorify God. Choose two or more of these possibilities
    and follow through with them this week.

# Digging Deeper

1. Study Matthew 5:17-48, Matthew 11:21-24, and Luke 12:47-48 in conjunction with James 2:10-11. Be sure to consider these verses in light of their context, and feel free to consult reputable commentaries. Then answer the following questions: Are all sins equally bad in God's sight? (For example, is driving 5 miles over the speed limit as reprehensible to God as idolatry or mass murder?) Is James teaching that all sins are equally bad? If not, what is he teaching? Does his teaching agree with that of Jesus? Discuss your answer with your pastor, one of your elders, or another knowledgeable church leader.

*"Yea, it is impossible to
separate works from faith,
as impossible to separate
burning and shining from fire."*

Martin Luther

# Chapter Four

# Back to Back

---

*What use is it, my brethren, if a man says he has faith, but he has no works? Can that faith save him? If a brother or sister is without clothing and in need of daily food, and one of you says to them, "Go in peace, be warmed and be filled," and yet you do not give them what is necessary for their body, what use is that? Even so faith, if it has no works, is dead, being by itself. But someone may well say, "You have faith, and I have works; show me your faith without the works, and I will show you my faith by my works." (James 2:14–18)*

If you are a fan of action-adventure stories, you no doubt can recall numerous examples of besieged heroes battling bravely against two-pronged attacks. Just last week on *Star Trek: Deep Space Nine*, I watched Sisko and Dax stand back to back in valiant defense against yet another Jem'Hadar ambush.

*Back to back*: It is a natural and effective defensive maneuver—and one that Paul and James used even more skillfully than Sisko and Dax. The enemies of Christianity are just as devious as those of the Federation, and they always approach on more than one front.

As Paul and James took up their weapons of pen and ink to carry out the orders of their Commander-in-Chief, they faced enemy soldiers charging from different directions. The battles these writers fought thus were radically different—but each battle was equally essential to winning the war. So as we study these verses in James's second chapter, remember that James is not fighting the same battle as Paul. He is, however, fighting the same war. Both writers are valiant in defending the truth of their God against the same vicious Enemy. But since they are battling in separate arenas, their dissimilar maneuvers should not be construed as assaults on each other.

### Useless Faith Doesn't Work

The Apostle Paul's battles in the war for God's truth are *primarily* waged against self-righteous legalists, whereas those of James are waged *primarily* against self-confident law-rejecters. Paul's usual enemies define Christianity in terms of a glorified checklist, whereas James's see Christianity as more of a glorified free-for-all. One group argues, "God saves those who keep His rules"; the other affirms, "Grace means never having to do anything at all." Both groups are wrong and stand condemned in Scripture by God's Holy Spirit.

The inspired writers of the New Testament all address these issues to some degree, but some writers emphasize one issue more than another. Paul is preoccupied with the dangers of legalism, and yet he speaks of a righteous God who, in judgment, "will render to every man according to his deeds" (Romans 2:5–6). He urges the Philippians to "work out [their] salvation with fear and trembling" (2:12), reminds the Ephesians that they were "created in Christ Jesus for good works" (2:10), and exhorts the Galatians not to "lose heart in doing good" (6:9).

He admonishes Timothy to "discipline [himself] for the purpose of godliness" (1 Timothy 4:7) and to "be diligent to present [himself] approved to God as a workman who does not need to be ashamed" (2 Timothy 2:15). He also warns Timothy to "flee from youthful lusts" and "refuse foolish and ignorant speculations" while pursuing "righteousness, faith, love and peace, with those who call on the Lord from a pure heart" (2 Timothy 2:22–23).

Paul assures Titus that God's grace is not based on "deeds which we have done in righteousness" (3:5) but nevertheless redeems the elect "from every lawless deed" and purifies for God "a people for His own possession, zealous for good deeds" (2:14). And he tells Philemon that although he has "enough confidence in Christ to order [him] to do that which is proper," he also has enough confidence in Philemon's faith to "know" that he will "do even more" than what Paul could have ordered (vv. 8, 21).

James, in the same way, sprinkles his exhortative defense of the good works of faith with definitive assertions of the grace of salvation. He speaks of a God "who gives to all men generously and without reproach" (1:5) and bestows "every good thing" and "every perfect gift" upon His elect (1:17). He explains that the elect of God were "brought . . . forth by the word of truth," not by their works (1:18), and that they were transformed in the process to be "doers of the word, and not merely hearers" (1:22).

James reminds his readers that God has been merciful to them, that His "mercy triumphs over judgment" (2:13), and that He "is opposed to the proud, but gives grace to the humble" (4:6). The grace of salvation, he says, enables endurance, and those who endure will see "that the Lord is full of compassion" (5:11).

James is no stranger to salvation by grace, but he knows that his readers are distorting its privileges. "What use is it, my brethren," he says, "if a man says he has faith, but has no works? Can that [kind of] faith save him?" Even though grace abounds where sin increases, it reigns in *righteousness*, not in death (Romans 5:20–21). God's pure and undefiled religion, received by grace through faith (Ephesians 2:8–9), *transforms* those it saves and changes them forever (2 Corinthians 5:17). The heart of stone melts into a heart of flesh, responsive to God's Spirit and eager to please Him (Ezekiel 11:19–20).

A person who *says* he has been changed but shows no evidence of transformation is either deceived himself or attempting to deceive others. Faith without works is not the child of pure and undefiled religion but the sign of an unregenerate heart still lost in sin. Faith that works to redeem the elect always produces redeemed works *in* the elect. The redeemed do not continue in sin that grace might increase (Romans 6:1); they put off the old self and strive to walk worthy of their high calling in Christ (Ephesians 4:1, 22–24). Their behavior reflects God's Spirit within them.

### Faith That Works Is Faith That Loves

Jesus told His disciples during their last night together, "By this all men will know that you are My disciples, if you have love for one another" (John 13:35). The

Apostle John, who was there that night, later proclaimed that "whoever has the world's goods, and beholds his brother in need and closes his heart against him, how does the love of God abide in him? Little children, let us not love with word or with tongue, but in deed and truth" (1 John 3:17–18). Peter, who also was there, encouraged believers, "Above all, keep fervent in your love for one another, because love covers a multitude of sins. Be hospitable to one another without complaint. As each one has received a special gift, employ it in serving one another, as good stewards of the manifold grace of God" (1 Peter 4:8–10).

Those foundational leaders who supported Christ's Church (Ephesians 2:19–22) understood the practical nature of the self-sacrificial, need-meeting love to which Jesus referred, and they passed on the concept to those who came after them. "Let love be without hypocrisy," Paul urges in Romans 12. "Be devoted to one another in brotherly love; give preference to one another in honor; . . . contributing to the needs of the saints, practicing hospitality" (vv. 9, 10, 13). And in 1 Corinthians 13, he defines love explicitly:

*Love is patient, love is kind, and is not jealous; love does not brag and is not arrogant, does not act unbecomingly; it does not seek its own, is not provoked, does not take into account a wrong suffered, does not rejoice in unrighteousness, but rejoices with the truth; bears all things, believes all things, hopes all things, endures all things. Love never fails (vv. 4–8a).*

Paul admonishes the wayward Corinthians to "pursue" love (14:1), indicating that it is more of an action than a feeling. He commends the Thessalonians for their love toward one another but encourages them to "excel still more" in this most excellent grace (1 Thessalonians 4:10).

Paul has no quarrel with James about faith's work of love. He probably would add a hearty "Amen!" to James's blunt statement, "If a brother or sister is without clothing and in need of daily food, and one of you says to them, 'Go in peace, be warmed and be filled,' and yet you do not give them what is necessary for their body, what use is that? Even so faith, if it has no works, is dead, being by itself" (2:15–17).

The beloved Apostle John summarizes the views of them both when he says in his first letter, "We know that we have passed out of death into life, because we love the brethren. He who does not love abides in death" (1 John 3:14). All three writers agree that the transforming nature of salvation in Christ works itself out in loving behavior.

### Faith Without Love Can't Save Your Soul

Faith without works is like an unloaded gun. It might *look* very impressive, but it cannot accomplish what it was designed to do. The faith that saves sinners transforms them in Christ Jesus to do good works—good works that will be seen by others, who then will glorify God (Ephesians 2:10; Matthew 5:16). Ephesians 1 tells us that God has saved the elect for the "praise of His glory" (vv. 6, 12, 14) and that those who are *known for their faith* are also known for their love (v. 15). The faith that saves sinners not only looks impressive; it is able to accomplish what it was designed to do. Regenerate people do much more than talk. Their faith works in love—and that praises God's glory.

James agrees with Paul's theology when he challenges his readers to " . . . 'show me your faith without the works, and I will show you my faith by my works'" (2:18). The grammatical structure of verse 18 has confounded scholars much brighter than I, so I'm not embarrassed to admit my inability to untangle it for you. Fortunately, understanding the argument contained in those sentences doesn't depend wholly on unsnarling their syntax. We don't have to know who's speaking to whom to hear James affirm the utter futility of trying to separate faith from love. Since both are graces produced by the regenerating power of pure and undefiled religion, they always will be found working together in the life of a believer.

A "faith" that speaks boldly but refuses to act declares most decisively that it is pure pretense. You may have heard the story of a performer named Blondin, who attracted a huge crowd one day in 1860 by crossing Niagara Falls several times on a tightrope. The people were so impressed with his skill that when he asked how many believed that he could cross again with a man on his shoulders, they all raised their hands. "Who wants to be first?" he enthusiastically queried. Then Blondin waited expectantly—while no one stepped forward. Like an unloaded gun, the crowd's professed faith was unable to accomplish its declared intention and thus proved itself to be only "impressive" pretense.

Thomas Manton, in his commentary on James, describes three elements of faith that testify to its genuineness by motivating action.[1] The first is the "strong principle" of God's love. Regenerated faith fills us with confident trust in the strength of God's love, which equips and enables us to love in return (1 John 4:7–21).

The second element is the "mighty aid" of God's Spirit. The redeemed are freed from fear to act out their faith because "the Spirit Himself bears witness with our spirit that we are children of God" (Romans 8:16). He "helps our weakness," "intercedes for us with groanings too deep for words" (v. 26), and "searches all things, even the depths of God" and reveals them to us (1 Corinthians 2:10), thus giving us "the mind of Christ" (v. 16).

The third element is the "high aim" of God's glory. The redeemed of the Lord are equipped and encouraged to fix their eyes on Jesus, lay aside every entangling encumbrance, and run with endurance the race set before them (Hebrews 12:1)—not for the purpose of self-exaltation, but to "offer to God an acceptable service with reverence and awe; for our God is a consuming fire" (vv. 28–29).

Once again Paul agrees fully with James. In his letter to Titus, he describes unfaithful Cretans whose lying, evil, and lazy behavior testify to the defilement and impurity of "both their mind and their conscience" (1:12, 15). "They profess to know God," Paul says to his colleague, "but by their deeds they deny Him, being detestable and disobedient, and worthless for any good deed" (v. 16).

Paul warns Timothy in similar language of men "holding to a form of godliness, although they have denied its power." He describes them as "evil men and impostors" who "proceed from bad to worse, deceiving and being deceived" (2 Timothy 3:1–5, 13). Timothy, as a man truly saved by grace through faith, is exhorted to "continue in the things [he has] learned and become convinced of, knowing from whom [he has] learned them" (v. 14) and to teach others to "love from a pure heart and a good conscience and a sincere faith" (1 Timothy 1:5).

Back to back in defense of God's truth, Paul and James stand "united in spirit and intent on one purpose" (Philippians 2:2) and would never even think of attacking each other. Although clearly engaging different enemy forces, they are, without doubt, fighting one war.

[1] Thomas Manton, *James. The Crossway Classic Commentaries.* Series eds. Alister McGrath and J. I. Packer (Wheaton, Ill.: Crossway Books, 1995), 145.

# Review Questions

1. Summarize in a few brief sentences your assurance that Paul and James are not fighting each other even though some of their statements sound contradictory. (Hint: Consider the opponents of Christianity that each writer is facing.)

2. Cite several examples of verses in which Paul agrees with what James says about "works."

3. What evidence do you see in James's letter that reveals his agreement with Paul on the issue of salvation by grace through faith?

4. Explain in your own words the connection between saving faith and works of love.

5. What is the ultimate purpose of the faith that saves sinners? Why is faith without works like an unloaded gun?

6. List and explain Thomas Manton's three elements of faith that testify to its genuineness by motivating action.

## Applying the Word

1. Give several specific examples of how the faith that worked to redeem you also produces redeemed works in you. Thinking about the following questions may help:

   What specific sins have you forsaken or decreased significantly since your salvation?

   What was your "old self" like? How does your new self differ from your old self? (Give specific examples of this difference.)

   What specific activities are you engaged in that reflect your desire to walk worthy of your high calling in Christ?

2.  Meditate upon how the "strong principle" of God's love, the "mighty aid" of God's Spirit, and the "high aim" of God's glory motivating your behavior as a Christian contribute to your assurance of salvation. Then summarize your insights as creatively as possible. Write a poem or a song; draw a picture or a diagram; or develop a lesson plan for teaching children, young people, or adults relating these three elements of faith to personal assurance. Ask God how He would have you use the results.

# Digging Deeper

1. Using this lesson as a pattern or guide, study the writings of one or more of the following New Testament writers: Luke, Peter, John, Jude, and the writer of Hebrews. Note examples of agreement between these men and James regarding the issues of salvation by grace through faith and the transformation of salvation that produces good works. Explain how your study has confirmed your assurance that all the New Testament writers indeed were fighting the same war while being "united in spirit" and "intent on one purpose."

*"Faith of the heart expresses itself through the deed of the hand."*

Simon J. Kistemaker

# Chapter Five

# Vital Signs of Spiritual Life

---

*You believe that God is one. You do well; the demons also believe, and shudder. But are you willing to recognize, you foolish fellow, that faith without works is useless? Was not Abraham our father justified by works, when he offered up Isaac his son on the altar? You see that faith was working with his works, and as a result of the works, faith was perfected; and the Scripture was fulfilled which says, "And Abraham believed God, and it was reckoned to him as righteousness," and he was called the friend of God. You see that a man is justified by works, and not by faith alone. And in the same way was not Rahab the harlot also justified by works, when she received the messengers and sent them out by another way? For just as the body without the spirit is dead, so also faith without works is dead. (James 2:19–26)*

When highly trained emergency medical technicians descend upon the scene of a serious accident, their second highest priority[1] is carefully evaluating the victim's "ABC's" (airway, breathing, and circulation), more commonly known as "vital signs." A person's vital signs reveal a great deal of significant information, not the least of which is whether he or she is alive or dead. If EMTs are unable to detect breathing and heartbeat, they assess the victim as "dead" and proceed accordingly. Even if they suddenly were to discover that the victim was wearing a T-shirt imprinted with the words I AM ALIVE!, their assessment and resulting procedures would not change. Such a declaration would be meaningless in the absence of "vital signs."

James never heard of an EMT, but in this passage he reminds me of one—in a spiritual sense. In assessing the presence of spiritual life in a professor, he looks for the presence of undeniably definitive "vital signs." The most vehement assertion of salvation's reality is tragically meaningless unless it is validated by these essential signs of spiritual life.

### Belief Alone Is Not Enough

D. Edmond Hiebert, in his commentary on James, says, "An inactive faith entombed in an intellectually approved creed, is of no more value than a corpse."[2] By shrouding "inactive faith" in the imagery of death, he paints an eloquent word picture of a faith that won't save.

This faith that won't save often is quite verbal. It talks loud and long about what it believes. It quotes theologians and long passages of Scripture while affirming, frequently in truth, its assent to pure orthodoxy. It builds for itself a dignified edifice resembling those of God's saints, which few people recognize as a well-disguised tomb.

This faith that won't save is belief without works—and it is the belief of the demons. The Bible teaches clearly that demons *believe* the truth about Christ. They know who He is and what His life means for us and for them. (See Mark

1:23–24 and Matthew 8:29.) Their belief in these truths brings them no comfort, however. Instead, it fills them with dread and leaves them shuddering in fear. Belief that stops short of redemptive salvation stands on the edge of a Godless eternity and stares without hope into the cruel mouth of hell.

One who says he has faith but produces no works reveals his alliance with demons rather than God. James can't find a pulse and detects no signs of breathing, even though the victim's garish T-shirt proclaims I AM ALIVE! James steps back from the body to study the scene closely and verify his suspicions. Yes . . . now he can see it. How very tragic: That dignified edifice of orthodox profession is, in reality, a well-disguised tomb. Spiritual life doesn't dwell there because it was built by a corpse.

### Abraham's Faith Was Justified by His Works

James validates his assertions regarding faith that can't save by citing an example that at first sounds quite shocking: "Was not Abraham our father justified by works, when he offered up Isaac his son on the altar?" (v. 21). Is James advocating salvation through the sacrifice of our children? No, he is not. His meaning becomes clear when we read the next two verses: "You see that faith was working with his works, and as a result of the works, faith was perfected; and the Scripture was fulfilled which says, 'And Abraham believed God, and it was reckoned to him as righteousness,' and he was called the friend of God."

Abraham's "work" of offering up his son on the altar did not save him. He had been saved long before—when he believed God's promise before his son was born (Genesis 15:1–6). God gave him the faith to believe what He said

(Ephesians 2:8–9) and then reckoned that faith to him as righteousness on the basis of what Christ would do when He came (2 Corinthians 5:21).

The faith that reckoned Abraham righteous also transformed him, and "was working with his works" so that his faith itself "was perfected." Abraham's "work of faith" testified that his faith indeed had saved him because it glorified God despite the cost to himself. Abraham had been changed by God's pure and undefiled religion. He had been liberated from the tyranny of self-centered behavior and enabled to act out his trust in the One who had saved him.

Hebrews 11:17 tells us that Abraham offered up Isaac "by faith." If Abraham had not had faith, he could not have done what he did. John Blanchard has said that "his faith was the energizing force that moved him to action" and that "his actions were the energetic evidence of his faith."[3] Faith and works simply cannot be separated. We can't do the good works for which God created us until He transforms us by His gracious salvation; and the works that result from our transformation in Christ tell the world and assure us that the faith we profess indeed has saved our souls.

Thus, says James, "You see that a man is justified by works, and not by faith alone." Faith that justifies (declares one righteous in God's sight) is a faith that transforms. And a faith that transforms is a faith that works. Faith that is alone—faith without works—is faith that cannot save, a faith that allies its professors with the demons, not God.

*And Furthermore, . . .*

James underscores his emphatic insistence upon the inseparability of faith and works by reminding his readers of Rahab—a Gentile prostitute whose works also proclaimed the reality of her faith.

Abraham and Rahab are a study in contrasts. He was an Israelite; she was a Gentile. He was upright and moral whereas she made her living as a practitioner of sin. He had walked long years with his God before called to Moriah, but she had only a few moments to prepare for her test in besieged Jericho.

The similarities of their faith outweigh all their differences, however. Both were chosen by God for redemption in Christ, and both were transformed to "work" for His glory. Abraham's test was no more difficult than hers, and her faith shines through her works just as brightly as his.

The lives of them both speak volumes about the faith that characterizes God's pure and undefiled religion. It's a faith that does more than declare I AM ALIVE! Its vital signs verify the truth of its words. Its airway is open to God's life-giving Spirit; its lungs work efficiently to exchange sin's pollution for scriptural truth; and every beat of its heart energizes body and soul to pursue loving obedience.

James's comparison of faith to our physical bodies is an apt illustration: "For just as the body without the spirit is dead, so also faith without works is dead" (v. 26). A spiritless body offers no signs of life—because the absence of spirit is the presence of death. In exactly the same way, an inactive faith denies the life of God's Spirit in the soul of the person. And the absence of God means spiritual death.

[1] Their highest priority is making sure they can safely enter the accident scene.

[2] D. Edmond Hiebert, *James* (Chicago: Moody Press, 1979, 1992), 179.

[3] John Blanchard, *Truth for Life: A Devotional Commentary on the Epistle of James* (Durham, England: Evangelical Press, 1986), 170.

# Review Questions

1. Describe the belief of demons. Include in your response a description of what demons believe about Jesus Christ and how they reacted when they encountered Him during His earthly ministry.

2. How does James relate the belief of demons to faith without works? Do you agree with him? Why or why not? Support your answer with Scripture.

3. When was Abraham "reckoned righteous" by God? Describe the events surrounding this "reckoning."

4. How does Abraham's willingness to sacrifice Isaac relate to his being reckoned righteous by God? What can you infer about Isaac's faith from this same incident? (Hint: See if you can determine Isaac's approximate age at the time of Abraham's offering and what that indicates about Isaac's participation in the sacrifice.)

5.  How was Rahab's faith similar to Abraham's?

---

6.  Explain the analogy James uses that associates the faith generated by God's pure and undefiled religion to the life that energizes a physical body.

## Applying the Word

1.  Thomas Manton, in his commentary on James, said that deeds
    without faith are just as useless as faith without deeds (p.
    154). Creatively explain this interrelationship between faith
    and deeds by writing a poem, short story, or skit; by drawing
    a picture or flowchart; or by composing a song. Use "real life"
    examples as illustrations if at all possible. Ask God how He
    would have you use the results.

2. Does your profession of faith align you with God, or with the demons? Explore this question by answering the ones that follow prayerfully, honestly, and specifically:

   What do you believe about Jesus Christ? (Who is He? What did He do? How did He do it? Where and when did He do it? Why did He do it?)

   How do your beliefs about Jesus impact your attitudes, emotions, and behavior? (Give specific examples.)

   What do your works say about your faith? (Cite specific examples of your works.)

3.  Suppose that you have just received the following letter from a friend you discipled several years ago:

> *Dear Friend and Spiritual Mentor,*
>
> *I am writing to let you know that I have begun to doubt the truth of Christianity. I have been reading the book of James and have discovered that he disagrees with the Apostle Paul about the nature of saving faith. Paul says in Romans 3:28, "For we maintain that a man is justified by faith apart from works of the Law," but James says in 2:24, "You see that a man is justified by works, and not by faith alone."*
>
> *You always taught me that God's Holy Spirit wrote the Bible through inspired writers-- but if that were true, these two writers would not be disagreeing with each other on such an important issue. How can I believe you when I find contradictions like these in the Bible?*
>
> *Sincerely,*
> *Your disillusioned friend*

Respond to your friend's letter and explain why the statements she quoted are not contradictory. Do any research necessary to answer her questions and address her concerns responsibly.

# Digging Deeper

1. Examine the Scriptural accounts of the professions of faith of people like Judas Iscariot and Simon the Sorcerer. (Use a concordance to find these accounts.) How does their professed faith compare with the faith professed by the likes of Paul, Peter, and John? What do the works of these people say about their profession of faith?

*"The power of man has grown
in every sphere
except over himself"*

∞

Sir Winston Churchill

# Chapter Six

# Taming a Tainted Tongue

---

*Let not many of you become teachers, my brethren, knowing that as such we shall incur a stricter judgment. For we all stumble in many ways. If anyone does not stumble in what he says, he is a perfect man, able to bridle the whole body as well. Now if we put the bits into the horses' mouths so that they may obey us, we direct their entire body as well. Behold, the ships also, though they are so great and are driven by strong winds, are still directed by a very small rudder, wherever the inclination of the pilot desires. So also the tongue is a small part of the body, and yet it boasts of great things. (James 3:1–5a)*

On the wall near my computer hangs a small, brightly colored poster that reads: "I know you believe you understand what you think I said, but I'm not sure you realize that what you heard is not what I meant." That little poster means a lot to me, primarily because it was a gift from a fellow teacher who has shared with me the many frustrations associated with the "ministry of communication." We both know that whenever one depraved (albeit redeemed) human being attempts to explain spiritual truth to other depraved (some redeemed; some not) human beings, misunderstanding and confusion inevitably result. And we often have surmised that Murphy must have a law that says, "If anything you say can possibly be misinterpreted, misapplied, twisted, or distorted—it will be."

Actually, teaching the Bible is much more than frustrating; it's downright terrifying. And if you don't think so, you have no business doing it. Interestingly enough, the terror of Bible-teaching doesn't reside in the size of your audience, or their intelligence, or their status. It does not arise from their status as friends, enemies, or strangers, nor does it lie in the degree of their alignment with your theological persuasion. It resides, instead, in the depraved inabilities of fallen human beings to communicate the perfect and powerful proclamations of God—and in the strict judgment imposed on those who communicate God's truth in an irresponsible manner.

### Think Before You Teach

Whenever I am privileged to teach and train teachers, I always begin with James 3:1: "Let not many of you become teachers, my brethren, knowing that as such we shall incur a stricter judgment." I do that to see if I can scare anyone off—because if I can, chances are good God hasn't called them to teach. And if He hasn't called them, they shouldn't be teaching.

Even though *all* Christians should be willing and able "to make a defense to everyone who asks you to give an account for the hope that is in you" (1 Peter 3:15), *not all* Christians should be willing (nor are they able) to accept *teaching positions* in the church. God has ordained that those positions be filled only by those He has specifically called, gifted, and equipped to shoulder the responsibility their influence entails. Pausing to ponder the magnitude of that responsibility is a good way to test the genuineness of a "call." Since teachers mold the thoughts and shape the behavior of saints who will, in turn, influence others, the "ministry of communication" has a ripple effect that intensifies every teacher's accountability before God.

Those who have genuinely experienced and acknowledged God's call to teach will be sobered—if not terrified—by the magnitude of the task, but rarely will they be dissuaded from pursuing it. They usually identify with Paul, who described his call as a "compulsion" (1 Corinthians 9:16), and they earnestly desire to "shine brightly like the brightness of the expanse of heaven" by "lead[ing] the many to righteousness" (Daniel 12:3) regardless of the high cost to themselves. They deeply appreciate the privilege of explaining God's truth creatively and practically, and they welcome the burden of handling it accurately through diligent study and careful preparation (2 Timothy 2:15).

They recognize that the goal of their instruction is "love from a pure heart and a good conscience and a sincere faith" (1 Timothy 1:5), so they seek to weave the 1 Corinthians 13 definition of love throughout all their endeavors. They teach with patience and kindness without holding grudges or being easily provoked. They guard against prideful self-exaltation and arrogant displays of "great learning." They pursue righteousness, love truth, and persevere in hope, no matter how discouraged or frustrated they may feel. The well-being of their students always takes precedence over "seeking their own." (See 1 Corinthians 13:4–8a.)

God-appointed teachers take the Apostle Paul seri-
ously when he admonishes them to practice what they
teach (Romans 2:21–23), and they pay close attention to the
counsel that Paul directs to Timothy, a fellow teacher of
truth. "If you want to be vessels of honor, set apart for God's
use," Paul says, in effect, in 2 Timothy 2:21–26, "then you
must flee from youthful lusts and pursue righteousness,
faith, love and peace, with those who call on the Lord from a
pure heart. You must refuse to engage in foolish and ignorant
discussions that generate quarrels while you teach lovingly
and kindly, remaining patient when you are wronged and
gently correcting those who oppose you."

God-appointed teachers thus are a study in contrasts.
Although they tremble at the thought of "speaking for God,"
they find it almost impossible to keep their mouths shut.
Martin Luther, one such teacher, collapsed while celebrating
his first Mass, overcome by the awesome sense of God's
thrice-holy presence. But that same sense of presence also
drove him to spark a world-shaking Reformation in the
handling of truth. A strange quaking boldness seemed to
characterize much of his ministry, exemplified clearly in
his stand before the Diet of Worms in April of 1521. His
courageous refusal to recant his incendiary writings came
after a dark night of struggle and closed with this anguished
and seemingly helpless appeal, "Here I stand. I cannot do
otherwise. God help me."[1]

Charles Spurgeon, perhaps England's greatest
nineteenth-century preacher, is said to have prayed desperately upon entering the pulpit, "O God, help!" He seemed
acutely aware of the absurd incongruity of God's truth being
delivered through the lips of a sinner.[2] And R. C. Sproul,
one of contemporary America's great preacher-teachers,

freely admits, "I cringe when I speak in churches about the holiness of God. . . . Because they hear me preach about holiness, they assume I must be as holy as the message I preach. That's when I want to cry, 'Woe is me.' . . . There is irony here. I am sure that the reason I have a deep hunger to learn of the holiness of God is precisely because I am not holy. I am a profane man—a man who spends more time out of the temple than in it. But I have had just enough of a taste of the majesty of God to want more. I know what it means to be a forgiven man and what it means to be sent on a mission. My soul cries for more. My soul needs more."[3]

Luther, Spurgeon, and Sproul reflect the hearts of all God-appointed teachers as they reveal their intimate acquaintance with the terror of teaching. They yearn after God's truth and seek to share it with others while agonizing over their fallen human propensity to stumble badly and often in the process—because they know that sharing God's truth requires using their tongues.

### *Every Sin in the Book*

Bible teachers aren't the only ones who struggle in agony with their stumblebum tongues. Most Christians I know marvel (in grief and horror) at how their tongues seem involved in "every sin in the book." The tongue kindles hatred, creates discord, generates confusion, incites lust, stirs up strife, and ruins reputations. That powerful little member is *essentially* involved in lying, swearing, scoffing, deception, quarreling, boasting, gossip, reviling, humiliation, poking fun, slander, blasphemy, coarse joking, harsh criticism, reproach, sarcasm, idle chatter, defamation, and contempt.

It's disheartening to realize how easily we sin when we open our mouths. But the reason that happens is really quite simple: Our words tend to reflect the conditions of our hearts (Matthew 12:34) which, according to Jeremiah, are "more deceitful than all else and [are] desperately sick" (17:9).

Although our salvation in Christ Jesus transformed our hearts from unresponsive stone to sensitive flesh, it did not leave them impeccable, or immune to temptation. They remain all too susceptible to the alluring beguilements of the world, the flesh, and the devil. And nowhere is that truth more clearly revealed than in our patterns of speech. Temptations that stimulate "sins of the heart" fester and grow in that fertile environment until they eventually spill out through our cooperative mouths. It's no wonder God saw fit to caution us in Proverbs to

> *Watch over your heart with all diligence,*
> *For from it flow the springs of life.*
> *Put away from you a deceitful mouth,*
> *And put devious lips far from you. (4:23–24)*

Controlling our tongues requires guarding our hearts. James says that a man who "does not stumble in what he says . . . is a perfect man [who is] able to bridle the whole body as well" (3:2). The word translated "perfect" in this verse, *teleios* in Greek, is used to refer to accomplishment, completion, or fulfillment, and it seems to be alluding to the sanctification process that works to conform us to the image of Christ. Complete conformity to that image awaits us in heaven; but as we mature in Christ here on earth, we begin to resemble Him more and more.

James's words, therefore, can be understood as both a caution and an encouragement. Since we will not achieve perfection in this life, we must guard our hearts diligently in order to refrain from sinning in our speech, but we must not lose hope in the effort "because greater is He who is in [us] than he who is in the world" (1 John 4:4). Every Christian has the perfect resource at his or her disposal to gain control over the seemingly unconquerable power of the sin-loving tongue.

### Getting the Situation Under Control

My family loves dogs and rarely has lived without at least one. We have owned dachshunds, cocker spaniels, and an interesting assortment of "pound puppies," all of whom we found remarkably easy to control. However, our most recent acquisition, a Chinese Shar-Pei named Dallas, has presented a most challenging contrast to her docile predecessors. Developed in China as guard dogs and fighters, her unusual-looking breed tends to be high-strung, independent, and extremely defensive. These dogs also are quite muscular and surprisingly strong for their size.

For two full years after we brought her home, walking Dallas seemed more like a wrestling match than a "good way to get a little exercise." But then a compassionate veterinarian introduced me to a marvelous device called a Gentle Lead. Obviously developed by other struggling-but-devoted owners of domineering dogs, it works wonders by applying pressure at two natural control points: the bridge of the nose and the scruff of the neck. With her head encased in this phenomenal contraption, Dallas becomes delightfully submissive, and my neighbors have stopped asking, "Who's walking whom?"

I wonder if the people who invented my lead got their idea from the bridle that's used to curb horses. These large, powerful animals present a much greater control challenge than my headstrong Shar-Pei, but they become quite compliant in response to a bit. Our good teacher, James, uses this excellent analogy to help us understand God's plan for controlling our recalcitrant tongues.

Few, if any, reasonable people would attempt to control a horse (or even my dog) by brute force alone. If they want to succeed, they reach for a device specifically designed to help them accomplish that task. In much the same way, Christians would be foolish to attempt control over their tongues without the specifically designed help of God's indwelling Spirit. Just as a bridle encourages compliance by applying pressure to sensitive areas, the Holy Spirit stimulates righteousness by applying pressure to our most sensitive area—the regenerated heart that has been softened by God. (See Romans 8:12–16, 26–27.)

When we "walk by the Spirit," we "will not carry out the desire of the flesh" (Galatians 5:16). When we are "filled with the Spirit," we will be able to speak righteously rather than sinfully (Ephesians 5:18–19). When we refrain from "quench[ing] the Spirit," we will be able to "hold fast to that which is good [and] abstain from every form of evil" (1 Thessalonians 5:19–22). And when we resist grieving the Spirit, we will let "no unwholesome word proceed from [our] mouth[s], but only such a word as is good for edification according to the need of the moment, that it may give grace to those who hear" (Ephesians 4:29).

A quick review of the long list of sins that require use of the tongue (page 217) should make it eminently clear that controlling our tongues will go a long way toward enabling us to glorify God more effectively as we walk more worthily of our high calling in Christ.

## Avoiding Disaster

Overconfidently thinking too highly of ourselves can be disastrous for Christians. When James adds emphasis to his teaching on tongue control by following his horse analogy with one about ships, I am reminded of the climactic scenes from the movie *Titanic*.

The *Titanic* was touted as an "unsinkable" ship, a prideful assertion dramatized in the movie by the wholesale overconfidence of the ship's owner and crew. J.Bruce Ismay, Chairman of the White Star Line, was determined to arrive in New York well ahead of schedule, and insisted on pushing the liner's huge engines to maximum speed. Captain Edward J. Smith, whose own overconfidence in the Titanic seemed to exacerbate his reputed indecisiveness, put up little resistance to Ismay's demands. The result of their arrogant disregard of wise sailing procedures was a tragedy of colossal proportions. "Great ships" can be controlled by a "very small rudder" (James 3:4); but when the fatal iceberg loomed into sight, the *Titanic* was simply moving too quickly to steer out of harm's way.

When we, in the same prideful manner, overconfidently neglect the wise precautions of tongue control, we can sink into sin just as quickly as the *Titanic* sank into the sea. Proverbs 10:19 warns us, "When there are many words, transgression is unavoidable, but he who restrains his lips is wise." Running our tongues at top speed is as dangerous to our spiritual welfare as was racing the *Titanic* through the icy North Atlantic to her physical safety.

Many factors contributed to the disastrous end of the *Titanic's* maiden voyage, all of which can be traced back to overconfident pride. Christians who want to steer wisely through the world's perilous waters would be wise to heed Paul's counsel found in Romans 12:3: "For   through the grace given to me I say to every man among you not to think more highly of himself than he ought to think; but to think so as to have sound judgment, as God has allotted to each a measure of faith."

[1]  Kenneth Scott Latourette, *A History of Christianity* (New York: HarperCollins Publishers, revised edition, 1975), Volume 2, 717.

[2]  Paul Lee Tan, *Encyclopedia of 7700 Illustrations: Signs of the Times* (Rockville, Md.: Assurance Publishers, 1985), 523.

[3]  R. C. Sproul, *The Holiness of God* (Wheaton, Ill.: Tyndale House Publishers, second edition, 1998), 33.

## Review Questions

1. Why is teaching the Bible a terrifying activity? List several ways in which a person might proclaim God's truth in an irresponsible manner.

2. What is the difference between being willing and able to explain the hope you have in Jesus Christ and accepting a teaching position in the church? Describe, in your own words, a person who genuinely has experienced and acknowledged God's call to teach and explain the responsibilities God places upon such a person.

3.  Refer to the list of sins that require use of your tongue on page
    217. See if you can categorize them by placing each one under
    one or more of the following headings:

<u>Kindles Hatred</u>

<u>Creates Discord</u>

<u>Generates Confusion</u>

<u>Incites Lust</u>

<u>Stirs Up Strife</u>

<u>Ruins Reputations</u>

4. Explain why James 3:2 is both a caution and an encouragement.

5. Relate James's horse and ship analogies to the biblical procedure for controlling our tongues. Be sure to include the work of God's Holy Spirit described in Galatians 5:16, Ephesians 4:29-30; 5:18-19, and 1 Thessalonians 5:19-22.

## Applying the Word

1.  Look back at your answer to Review Question 2 and prayer-
    fully consider whether that description is a description of
    you. Have you experienced and acknowledged God's call to
    teach? If so, describe your call and response to it. What kind of
    activities are you pursuing to fulfill your call? Describe your
    feelings (your emotions, not your thoughts) about teaching
    God's truth and your commitment to your task. Then describe
    some blessings and some frustrations you have experienced
    in your work.

    If you have *not* been called by God to teach, what kind of
    "unofficial, teaching type" activities should you be willing
    to pursue? Give some specific examples of these types of
    activities and a few personal examples of opportunities God
    has given you to pursue them.

2. Using both a standard and a Bible dictionary, write your own definition of the following sins:

lying:


swearing:


scoffing:


deception:


quarreling:


boasting:


gossip:


reviling:


humiliation:

poking fun:


slander:


blasphemy:


coarse joking:


harsh criticism:


reproach:


sarcasm:


idle chatter:


defamation:


contempt:

Give several specific, personal examples of times when you have committed at least five of these sins. In each case, think about and describe whether committing the sin kindled hatred, created discord, generated confusion, incited lust, stirred up strife, or ruined someone's reputation. Prayerfully consider whether you need to repent of these sins (and you do if you haven't already!) and whether you need to seek forgiveness and reconciliation with someone against whom you have sinned. If so, follow through!

Finally, use a concordance to find several verses that describe how you can avoid committing these kinds of sins in the future. (An example of such a verse would be Ephesians 4:29.) Memorize at least two such verses.

# Digging Deeper

1. Using a concordance, expository dictionary, and any other useful study aids at your disposal, do a word study on the Greek word *teleios*. Then use what you have learned in your study to refute the following statement: "Controlling our tongues is impossible; therefore, it is foolish to attempt to do so. James says that only a perfect person can do it, and none of us will be perfect until we get to heaven. Since God's grace covers all our sins, we have nothing to worry about. So why waste the energy?"

*"A sharp tongue is the only edged tool that grows keener with constant use."*

∞

Washington Irving

# Chapter Seven

# *Who Does Your Tongue Say You Are?*

---

*Behold, how great a forest is set aflame by such a
small fire! And the tongue is a fire, the very world
of iniquity; the tongue is set among our members
as that which defiles the entire body, and sets on
fire the course of our life, and is set on fire by hell.
For every species of beasts and birds, of reptiles
and creatures of the sea, is tamed, and has been
tamed by the human race. But no one can tame
the tongue; it is a restless evil and full of deadly
poison. With it we bless our Lord and Father; and
with it we curse men, who have been made in the
likeness of God; from the same mouth come both
blessing and cursing. My brethren, these things
ought not to be this way. Does a fountain send out
from the same opening both fresh and bitter water?
Can a fig tree, my brethren, produce olives, or a
vine produce figs? Neither can salt water produce
fresh. (James 3:5b–12)*

The story is told of the heathen philosopher Xanthus
who, in preparing a dinner for several close friends, ordered
his servant Aesop to scour the marketplace for the best
possible victuals. Aesop obediently scoured and returned

with a basket filled with nothing but tongues.

The guests seemed amused by course after course of creatively prepared tongues, but Xanthus was furious. "Didn't I order you to buy the market's best victuals for my dear treasured friends? How dare you set before them nothing but tongues!"

Aesop replied, "But have I not perfectly fulfilled your orders? Does the market hold any finer treasure than tongues? Tongues form the bond of civil society; they are the organ that proclaims all reason and truth. And they declare both our esteem for all men and our praise of the gods."

"Well said," Xanthus responded. "But I have invited my guests to return at the same time tomorrow. And I order you then to bring to my table the market's very *worst* victuals." Aesop complied, and the friends of Xanthus dined the next day on *the very same fare.*

"What! Tongues again?" Xanthus raged at his servant.

"Of course," said wise Aesop. "The market also contains nothing worse than the tongue. It produces strife and contention; it instigates lawsuits. It creates division and wars, and it spreads lies, error, and slander. It ruins the reputations of men while it blasphemes the gods. Surely in the whole world, there exists nothing worse than the tongue."[1]

The insightful servant of Xanthus couldn't have been more right. The power of the tongue determines the direction of people's lives as well as the course of history—and it wields its influence for both good and evil.

This fact is illustrated well by the stunning impact of two powerful men on the world: John Knox and Adolf Hitler. Mary, Queen of Scots, once said she feared the tongue of John Knox more than an army of 10,000 men—and with very good reason. His biblical preaching fueled truth-illuminating fires of Reformation throughout Scotland that not even her considerable power could extinguish. Knox thus used his tongue to accomplish great good, whereas, in much the same way but for a much different purpose, Adolf Hitler used his tongue to serve Satan's forces of darkness.

An apt epitaph befitting the legacy of both men could have been borrowed from the words penned by James in the text of our lesson: "Behold, how great a forest is set aflame by such a small fire!" (3:5).

### A Distorted Image

Scripture tells us that God created human beings *in His image* so that they could glorify Him in particular ways (Genesis 1:26–27; Isaiah 43:7). Even though the whole of creation glorifies God, men and women have been blessed with a much greater capacity to glorify Him uniquely. No rock, hill or mountain; no meadow or plain; no ocean or sea, lake, river, or stream can speak of God's attributes or exalt Him in song as we humans can.[2]

Our ability to think, reason, and speak equips us for fellowship with God and each other. And God designed us that way to maximize His own glory. Whereas nature declares His power, perfection, and magnificence by its very existence, it has not been made capable of revealing God's heart. That privilege is ours because we have been made *verbal*.

Tragically, however, our first parents freely chose to spurn that great privilege and sin against God. That incomprehensible and indefensible decision left indelible marks on all of their children, the most glaring of which may very well be its effect on our tongues. The second human sentence recorded after man's ejection from Eden was a lie told to God to cover a crime (Genesis 4:9). And when the righteous prophet Isaiah was driven to his knees in repentance by a splendid vision of God, he saw clearly his own sinfulness reflected in the light of God's glory and framed his confession in terms of the things that routinely came out of his mouth:

*"Woe is me, for I am ruined!*
*Because I am a man of unclean lips,*
*And I live among a people of unclean lips;*
*For my eyes have seen the King, the LORD of hosts."*
*(Isaiah 6:5)*

The reason "the tongue is a fire . . . which defiles the entire body" is because we are sinners in whom the image of God has been grossly distorted. Distortion always inhibits intended purpose and function; that's why our tongues are more prone to "[set] on fire the course of our life" than to speak in exaltation of the glory of God. The words of Jesus in Matthew 12:34 remind us that "the mouth speaks out of that which fills the heart," and Jeremiah makes clear that our hearts are "more deceitful than all else and [are] desperately sick" (17:9).

We saw in the previous chapter that our salvation in Christ Jesus transformed our sick hearts but did not make them impervious to sinful appeals from the world, the flesh, and the devil. Although we now are free, in God's Spirit, from sin's controlling power, we still can choose to submit to tempation. God designed salvation this way for the praise of His glory. If we could resist sin and obey God in our strength alone, the praise for those actions would accrue to us instead of to Him. But because we remain weak in our flesh, even as regenerated saints, we must depend on the Spirit to follow God's call and obey His commands.

Even though "every species of beasts and birds, of reptiles and creatures of the sea . . . has been tamed by the [fallen] human race," no human being can tame his own tongue—without help from God's Spirit. That help won't even be sought unless the heart has been supernaturally softened and filled with the desire to please its Redeemer. But when saved saints seek His help and acknowledge His work, the resultant display of speech under control gives glory to God and to the work of His Son.

### Fulfilling Your Purpose

James's words in our text proclaim the unsettling truth that in all the natural realm, only humanity acts contrary to the purpose for which God created it. Fountains don't pour out both fresh water and bitter, nor is salt water found intermingled with sweet. Fig trees don't produce olives, nor do olive vines bear figs. Only human beings, whose powers of speech were intended to proclaim the glories of God, spew forth cursing incompatible with such adoration and praise.

Sin caused that disparity, and only salvation can heal it. But fulfilling the purpose of God's gracious election requires us to work also. Although our hearts have been sensitized to conviction and truth, they are still drawn toward the temptations that abound in this world. James warns us explicitly that even redeemed tongues "bless our Lord . . . and curse men," that "from the same mouth come both blessing and cursing," and that "these things ought not to be this way." Those who love God because they have been redeemed as His children must draw on the power of the Spirit within them to speak in a manner that reflects who they are.

The pure and undefiled religion that God reveals in His Word, studied and applied in the power of His Spirit, is all that we need to get our tongues under control. When our hearts are steeped in His glorious truth and our thoughts congregate at the foot of the Cross, our tongues will clearly proclaim to the world who we really are.

---

[1] Adapted from Paul Lee Tan, *Encyclopedia of 7700 Illustrations: Signs of the Times* (Rockville, Md.: Assurance Publishers, 1979), 1423.

[2] See Psalm 19 for a description of how the created universe glorifies God without speech, words, or voice whereas men and women glorify Him by understanding and communicating God's truth in the "words of [their] mouth[s] and the meditations of [their] heart[s]."

# Review Questions

1. Paraphrase James 3:5b-12, emphasizing the power of the tongue to generate both good and evil.

2. Describe the important truth about Scripture reflected in the examples of the influence of John Knox's preaching and Adolf Hitler's oratory in conjunction with our text in this lesson.

3.  Read and study Genesis 1:26-27 and Isaiah 43:7. What do these
    passages tell you about the creation of the human race?




4.  Read and study the following passages of Scripture. In the
    space provided, summarize the teaching of each one.

Genesis 3:1-4:9:


Job 38:1-7; 40:1-5; 42:1-6:


Isaiah 6:1-5:


Jeremiah 17:9:


Ezekiel 11:19-21; 36:22-27:


Matthew 12:34-37; 15:15-20;


Colossians 4:6:


James 1:19-25; 3:2-12:

5. Using your answers to Review Question 4 along with what you have learned from Chapters Six and Seven, explain the connection between the tongue and the heart.

6. What part does God's Holy Spirit play in taming our tongues?

## Applying the Word

1. Describe one or more specific examples of your own inability to tame your tongue before you were transformed in Christ Jesus. Then give several specific examples of your failures to control your tongue since your redemption. Do you see any qualitative differences in these sins? (In other words, do you sin *differently* now from the way in which you sinned before?) From your personal knowledge of Scripture, can you explain why you see (or do not see) any difference in your "before" and "after" sins of the tongue?

   Now prayerfully read Paul's words in Ephesians 4:1-6 and 4:11-5:2. Describe why Paul believes "taming the tongue" is an essential endeavor for Christians. Go through these verses again and record those that convict you about specific sins of speech in your life. Then make a plan of action to deal with those sins and share it with someone who loves you enough to hold you accountable.

Read 2 Corinthians 9:8, Philippians 4:13, and John 4:1-4. Then describe the *hope* you find in those verses that will encourage you as you seek to tame your tongue according to the example of Christ, in the power of the Spirit, and to the glory of God.

2. Summarize the essential message of James 1:21-3:12 and list at least five specific applications you will make in your life on the basis of this passage of Scripture. Then describe in detail how you will implement at least one of your applications.

# Digging Deeper

1. Using a concordance, expository dictionary, and other reliable theological references, research and write a descriptive analysis of the way in which each member of the Trinity participates in salvation to justify and transform God's elect. Then describe why and how the work performed by each member of the Trinity relates both to the *necessity* and *ability* of saints controlling their tongues.

# James on
# Wisdom

How Faith Produces Sensible Living

James 3:13-5:20

## Carol Ruvolo

*"Wisdom's ways alone
are ways of pleasantness,
and wisdom's paths alone
are paths of peace."*

J.C. Ryle

*Faith at Work*
*Studies in the Book of James*
# Volume III

*For Carol Meyers,*

*whose gentle and quiet spirit*
*is rooted deep in God's wisdom.*

# Introduction

## *The Wisdom of Sensible Living*

---

When Paul wrote his New Testament letter to Titus, he described God's purpose for redeeming His chosen: " . . . that He might redeem us from every lawless deed and purify for Himself a people for His own possession, zealous for good deeds" (2:14). His words affirm those of the Westminster divines, who declared the chief end of man to be glorifying God and enjoying Him forever.[1]

If you have worked through the first two books in the *Faith at Work* series, you know that James brings into sharp focus the connection between the good works of redemption and the "chief end" of God's chosen. He emphasizes that "faith without works is dead" (2:17) because faith is revealed by the works that we do (vv. 14–26). James echoes the words of his brother Jesus, who told His disciples, "Let your light shine before men in such a way that they may see your good works, and glorify your Father who is in heaven" (Matthew 5:16). If you read Jesus' words quickly because you've seen them before, please go back and read them again slowly and thoughtfully. When I did that just now, I was struck by the phrase *in such a way*. Apparently we can "let our light shine" in ways that do not glorify God!

In fact, Jesus deals with this very issue a few verses later. In Matthew 6:1, He warns us, "Beware of practicing your righteousness before men *to be noticed by them"* (italics added for emphasis). Obviously Jesus is not saying that we should always practice our righteousness secretly, because if we did, men could not see our good works and glorify God. Rather, Jesus is warning us against practicing our righteousness in such a way as to draw attention to ourselves rather than God. The great Puritan teacher Thomas Manton expressed it this way: "It is one thing to do works that can be seen and another to do works in order that they shall be seen."[2] God is glorified when our shining light of good works illumines His character for those around us to see.

How in the world can we do that effectively? Paul's letter to Titus gives us a concise answer that will serve as our launching pad for this third study of James. Paul says that God's grace has brought us salvation, "instructing us to deny ungodliness and worldly desires and to live sensibly, righteously and godly in the present age" (Titus 2:11–12).

So how in the world do we glorify God with our good works? First of all, we do it *in the world*—or "in the present age." All of creation "naturally" glorifies God—except fallen humanity. (See Romans 1:20–23.) Only those human beings who have been transformed by God's Spirit through the work of salvation (1 Corinthians 2:6–16) have the desire and the ability to glorify Him instead of themselves. One of the reasons He leaves Christians *in the world* after we're saved is to grant us the joyous privilege of living out His created purpose for people.

Secondly, we glorify God with our good works by denying ungodliness and worldly desires. Even though salvation transforms us, it does not eliminate our ability or desire to sin. God left us vulnerable to the snares of the world, the flesh, and the devil so that we would have to depend upon Him to resist temptation. Thus, when we successfully deny ungodliness and worldly desires, He gets the glory—not us. Paul explained it to the Corinthians like this: "But we have this treasure [the testimony of the Gospel] in earthen vessels, that the surpassing greatness of the power may be of God and not from ourselves" (2 Corinthians 4:7).

And thirdly, we glorify God by our good works when we "live sensibly, righteously, and godly." Most of us understand that righteous and godly living involves keeping God's commandments and following the example set for us by Christ and the apostles (1 Peter 1:14–16; 1 John 2:3–6; 1 Corinthians 11:1). But what does Paul mean when he tells us to live *sensibly*? I must admit to being stumped when I asked myself that question a few days ago. So I dusted off my trusty dictionary and looked up the word *sensible*. Here's what I found: "having or showing wisdom or common sense; reasonable; judicious."[3] Sensible living involves living *wisely*, which is what the book of James is all about.

Many of the commentators I've read label the epistle of James as the "wisdom literature of the New Testament." That's because "wisdom literature" concerns practical issues of life. It takes the great truths of God and applies them to the nitty-gritty of daily events. Even though all of Scripture is useful because of its relevance to real-life situations (2 Timothy 3:16–17; 2 Peter 1:3), a few books of the Bible focus intensely on those practical issues. The wisdom literature of the Old Testament includes Job, Proverbs, and Ecclesiastes; and the outstanding New Testament example is the book of James.

I'm sure you remember that James was the leader of the first-century Church at the time it was dispersed abroad as a result of severe persecution in Jerusalem (Acts 8:1). The scattered Christians faced many difficulties and trials while living in foreign lands; and James, their compassionate leader, wrote the letter we are studying to encourage them with a reminder of the worth of their faith.

He began "where they were" with a rousing discussion of how Christian faith "works" in trials (James 1:2–25). He reminds his suffering brethren that they have all they need *in their faith* to face any difficulty *in such a way* that God will be glorified and they will have joy. But faith's work in trials is not automatic; it requires activation. That happens when individual Christians prove themselves doers of the Word and not merely hearers. This was the subject of the first book in our study, *James on Trials.*

James then broadens his focus a bit and explains why Christian faith works so well in trials (James 1:26–3:12). The saving faith that redeemed us also transformed us. And redeemed transformation produces good works (such as righteous responses to trials) that glorify God (Isaiah 43:7) and deepen our joy (Psalm 37:3–5) by fulfilling our created purpose (Psalm 35:9, 27–29; Ephesians 2:8–10). We looked at these characteristics of saving faith in the second book in our study, *James on Works.*

As we embark on the third and final book in our study of James's letter, we will see him broaden his focus still more. In 3:13–5:20, James explains that the characteristics of saving faith that "work" so well in trials "work" equally well in every situation of life. The saving faith that transforms us through Christ's redemption is our source of wisdom for sensible living.

[1] *The Shorter Catechism with Scripture Proofs*. Carlisle, PA: The Banner of Truth Trust, nd, 1.

[2] Thomas Manton, *The Crossway Classic Commentaries: James*. Series editors Alister McGrath and J. I. Packer (Wheaton, Ill.: Crossway Books, 1995), 202.

[3] *The Oxford Dictionary and Thesaurus,* New York: Oxford University Press, American edition (1996), s. v. "sensible."

*"True wisdom shows itself generally
in every part of a man's life
and especially in that wise gentleness
that comes from a proper conception of God
as the Creator
who stands at the beginning of things,
as the Faithful One
who overrules the present,
and as the Judge
who is utterly in control of the future."*

John Blanchard

# Chapter One

# Wise or Pseudo-Wise?

---

*Who among you is wise and understanding? Let him show by his good behavior his deeds in the gentleness of wisdom. But if you have bitter jealousy and selfish ambition in your heart, do not be arrogant and so lie against the truth. This wisdom is not that which comes down from above, but is earthly, natural, demonic. For where jealousy and selfish ambition exist, there is disorder and every evil thing. But the wisdom from above is first pure, then peaceable, gentle, reasonable, full of mercy and good fruits, unwavering, without hypocrisy. And the seed whose fruit is righteousness is sown in peace by those who make peace. (James 3:13–18)*

If you have ever worked at a job that involved handling cash, you have probably been trained to recognize counterfeit currency. Although your training program may have differed from the one I went through, the goal of them both was most likely the same: equipping employees to spot phony money.

Your employer and mine expended valuable company resources to make sure we developed this particular skill, and they would not have done so without a good reason. Failure to recognize counterfeit money almost always results in financial loss to the company. In businesses that handle large volumes of cash, such losses can be substantial if employees aren't good at detecting forgeries. A person or company that accepts a counterfeit bill cannot take it to the Treasury Department and exchange it for a real one. As soon as a counterfeit is unmasked, its owner loses. That's why wise business managers train their employees to distinguish between fake and real money. They know that such an investment will pay off in the long run.

James might have been such a wise businessman in his home town of Nazareth. Since his name comes first in two biblical lists of Jesus' brothers (Matthew 13:55; Mark 6:3), he was probably the eldest of them–the one who would have taken over the family business when Jesus left home to begin His ministry. No doubt, he encountered some counterfeit money.

Being able to spot pseudo-money would have been important to him, and may have helped him see the much greater value of recognizing pseudo-wisdom. James therefore devotes almost half of his letter to equipping his readers to excel in this skill. In 3:13–18, he defines for them the difference between true and false wisdom. And in 4:1–5:20, he fleshes out his description with real-life examples.

### Unmasking Deception

Any valuable commodity is subject to counterfeit. Greed and self-interest are not only creative but highly industrious. Every year talented, diligent forgers work overtime to turn out excellent replicas of not only money but also great paintings, fine jewels, and brand-name wearing apparel. Why do they do it? Why not pour all that time and energy into honest endeavors? Obviously, the forgers believe they have more to gain by trafficking in deception. In their minds, crime not only pays; it pays very well.

Counterfeiting is lucrative because most people fall for it. Forgers count on the fact that you and I cannot distinguish between a real twenty-dollar bill, a real Rembrandt, a real diamond, or even a real pair of Reeboks®, and an imitation. That kind of discernment requires training that most folks don't have. The profit in this kind of crime comes when the deceiver is more skilled in his craft than are the deceived at protecting themselves.

None of us want to suffer the losses that result from falling prey to deception in this material realm. Defending ourselves requires some effort however. Before we can foil an artful forger, we must acquire specialized knowledge of the things in which we are dealing. Wise living involves knowing the difference between the real and the fake.

If this is true in the material world, it is even more true in the spiritual. Being taken in by our enemy, whom Scripture describes as a deceiver (Revelation 12:9) and the father of lies (John 8:44), is a great deal more serious than paying too much for a phony Picasso. Satan works most effectively to disrupt God's purposes by deceiving His saints. He disguises himself as an angel of light and tries to pass off his counterfeit wares as God's genuine articles. One of those wares is counterfeit wisdom. If we don't want to be duped, we must know the difference between it and God's wisdom.

"Who among you is wise and understanding?" James

asks his readers. "Let him show by his good behavior his deeds in the gentleness of wisdom" (James 3:13). James wants those who believe that they are wise to examine themselves to see if they have been fooled. True wisdom is an attribute of God (Job 12:13) that He communicates to His people (Proverbs 8:33; Ephesians 5:15). _Gentleness_ is a synonym for "humble" or "meek," which when used in regard to a Christian, describes a person whose willing submission to God's authority springs from confident trust in His loving sovereignty.[1]

Therefore, if our "good behavior" reflects both our Father's righteousness and our contentment in His perfect care, we can count ourselves undeceived and genuinely wise. Before we can draw that conclusion, however, we must examine ourselves with the help of God's Holy Spirit (Psalm 139:23–24). Satan's craftiness extends beyond his initial attempts to sell us fake wisdom; he also capitalizes on our propensity for self-justification whenever we seek to analyze our behavior.

That is why James couples wisdom with _understanding_. The Greek word he uses may be applied to someone who is an expert in a particular field. It describes a person who has gained deep knowledge of a subject through observation and study.[2] The ability to distinguish between real and fake wisdom requires such understanding—a deep knowledge of God and of the ways in which He works. J. I. Packer expressed it this way: "Not until we have become humble and teachable, standing in awe of God's holiness and sovereignty . . . acknowledging our own littleness, distrusting our own thoughts, and willing to have our minds turned upside down, can divine wisdom become ours."[3]

This kind of knowledge is available only to those who have been adopted into God's family through redemption in Christ. All the wisdom of God is embodied in Christ, and our union with Him opens it to us (1 Corinthians 1:30; Colossians 2:2–3). As the Holy Spirit stimulates us to commune with our Father through Bible study and prayer, our understanding of Him grows deeper and stronger (Psalm 119:97–99; 1 Corinthians 2:14–16). And this understanding motivates us to live "in the gentleness of wisdom"—to behave in ways that reflect both our Father's righteousness and our humble submission to His loving authority (Proverbs 3:5–7; Galatians 5:16).

### *Wisdom from Below*

When James wrote his epistle to the dispersed first-century Christians, he knew that many of them were unwise and behaving accordingly. He also knew that although unwise believers cannot lose their salvation (Romans 8:1), neither can they live out God's purpose for their redemption. God adopts children and calls them by His name so that they will display His glory and have fullness of joy (Isaiah 43:7; Psalm 37:4–6; John 15:8–11). Christians who aren't practicing "good deeds in the gentleness of wisdom" can do neither of those things with any degree of effectiveness.

When Christians fail to fulfill God's purpose for them, they play into the hands of the prince of this world. Although Christ's work on the cross broke Satan's power and marked his defeat (John 12:30–33), it did not render believers immune to his crafty devices. Satan's hatred for God is so intense that even Christ's triumph on Calvary hasn't dimmed his desire to derail God's plans. Since we are God's children, we should not be surprised that he targets us.

Since his power to control us is gone, Satan resorts to deception. He can't force us to serve him, but he can delude us into believing that his ways are God's. He does that when he sells us counterfeit wisdom. When he successfully cloaks "bitter jealousy and selfish ambition" (James 3:14) in the guise of God's wisdom, he sows seeds of discord in the Church that obscure God's glory and shackle our joy. Christians who buy Satan's lie end up exchanging good deeds motivated by humble knowledge of God for self-centered activities driven by envy of others and desire for advancement. They operate according to a "wisdom" James tells us "is not . . . from above, but is earthly, natural, demonic" (v. 15).

Many commentators on James have noted the *progression* away from God and His purposes in this description. Earthly wisdom is concerned with the temporal instead of the eternal; natural wisdom is grounded in human potential, not that of the Spirit; and *demonic* wisdom is committed to Satan's agenda rather than God's. James's assessment of counterfeit wisdom aligns itself well with the New Testament's depiction of the three sources of temptation that trouble us as Christians: the world, the flesh, and the devil.

Earthly wisdom pulls us a few steps from God by riveting our attention on the good things in the world. Instead of counting the cost and being willing to sacrifice comfort and ease in pursuit of the Kingdom, we begin to see faith in Christ as our ticket to temporal bliss. Natural wisdom drags us even further from God by assuring us that the temporal success we desire actually depends on our fleshly efforts. We begin to believe we can achieve more in a life apart from God than we can in a life imparted by Him.[4]

And demonic wisdom drives us far away from our Father as it drips Satan's venom into our minds: *God doesn't love us. He is just using us. We should defend ourselves by working against Him.* Do you see how progressive counterfeit wisdom walks hand in hand with progressive temptation?

When we allow Satan to sell us his bill of goods, we give "jealousy and selfish ambition" free rein to incite "disorder and every evil thing" (v. 16) in the body of Christ. And where such things abound, God's glory and our joy will not be able to thrive.

### Wisdom from Above

Genuine wisdom is a gift of God. He gives it to us, His children, when He adopts us in Christ. Since "all the treasures of wisdom and knowledge" are hidden in Christ (Colossians 2:3), and our lives as believers are "hidden with Christ in God" (3:3), God's wisdom in Christ is at our disposal. This wisdom is incomprehensible to unbelievers but is "freely given to us" through the work of His Spirit (1 Corinthians 2:6–14). Since we have been blessed with "the mind of Christ" (v. 16), we have no excuse for succumbing to Satan's devices. If we are to live out the purpose for which God redeemed us, our attitudes, actions, and thinking must be controlled by the wisdom that is "from above" (James 3:17).

James says that this kind of wisdom "is first pure, then peaceable, gentle, reasonable, full of mercy and good fruits, unwavering, without hypocrisy" (v. 17)—a masterful description that identifies wisdom's essence as well as its effects. It is "first pure"—that is, pristine and unstained by the world, the flesh, and the devil. In other words, it is thoroughly God's. It comes from God to us through the work of His Son.

The word *then* in James's description marks a transition from wisdom's essence to its effects. As we rely on God's Spirit to illumine God's Word, His wisdom motivates our soft hearts to live out His purpose for us (Ezekiel 11:19–20; 36:26–27). Our *attitudes* toward the circumstances of life become peaceable, gentle, and reasonable. Our *behavior* begins to be marked by mercy and goodness. And our *thinking* is characterized less and less by hypocrisy and more and more by unwavering devotion to God and His purposes.

What happens when Christians operate according to God's pure wisdom instead of Satan's counterfeit? James says, "the seed whose fruit is righteousness is sown in peace by those who make peace" (v. 18). The syntax of this verse has confounded biblical scholars much brighter than I am, so please forgive my reluctance to unscramble it for you. However, there are two things we can know simply by reading this verse. Those who live in accordance with the pure wisdom of God (1) will reflect God's righteousness to those around them and (2) will be used of God in the role of peacemaker—to make peace between individuals and between God and sinners. Both of these activities glorify God in the world and stimulate joy in our relationship with Him—the very purposes for which He has saved us.

Fulfilling our purpose as God's chosen children requires us to live *wisely*. And as we continue to study the rest of his letter, we'll see James (true to form) describe many practical ways in which we can do that.

[1] John MacArthur, Jr., *The MacArthur New Testament Commentary: James* (Chicago: Moody Press, 1998), 169.

[2] Blanchard, *Truth for Life*, 201.

[3] *Ibid.*, 202.

[4] I borrowed the memorable phrasing of this sentence from D. Edmond Hiebert, *James* (Chicago: Moody Press, 1979, 1992), 204.

## Review Questions

1. If you have received training designed to equip you to recognize counterfeits, describe this training. Why was it important for you to develop this skill? How does this life experience help you understand the importance of developing skill in recognizing spiritual counterfeits? Explain your answer, using scriptural references to support your understanding. If you have not received this kind of training, how has reading this lesson helped you understand the importance of developing skill in recognizing spiritual counterfeits? Support your answer with Scripture.

2. What is *wisdom*? Consult both a standard dictionary and a biblical or theological dictionary; then write a definition of wisdom in your own words. Be sure to explain the connection between wisdom and understanding.

3. Describe the *alignment* between the progression of temptation (the world, the flesh, and the devil) and the progression of counterfeit wisdom (earthly, natural, and demonic).

4. What is the essence of God's wisdom? What are its effects? How does living in accordance with God's wisdom influence our attitudes, our actions, and our thinking?

5. List the words that James uses in 3:17 to describe God's wisdom. Consider these words, consulting a standard dictionary, a biblical or theological dictionary, and commentaries on James. Then, in your own words, write a clear, concise definition for each of the words that you listed. After you have done so, expand your answer to Review Question 4 to include insights that you may have gained from working on these definitions.

6. What happens when Christians operate by God's pure wisdom instead of by Satan's counterfeit? (Hint: See James 3:18.) What is the significance of what happens?

## Applying the Word

1. In his commentary on James, D. Edmond Hiebert highlights the deviousness of Satan's tactics when he says, "Religious zeal or enthusiasm for God and truth is a commendable attitude, but the subtleties of sinful human nature can readily pervert it into bitter antagonism against those who do not express their adherence to God and His truth in the same way we do." (See footnote on page 261; this quotation appears on page 206 of that work.) List one or more specific examples (from your own experience, if possible) that illustrate Hiebert's statement. Then reread James 3:14–16 and explain how these examples reveal Satan's devious tactics at work to "sell" us counterfeit wisdom. Make a plan of action to defend yourself against these devious tactics and share it with someone who loves you enough to hold you accountable.

2.  Reread your answer to review question #5. Then give a specific example of how you can begin implementing each "effect" of pure wisdom in your life this week. (In other words, what *specific* things must you stop doing and begin doing in order to make your attitudes more peaceable, gentle, and reasonable; your actions more merciful and good; and your thinking less hypocritical and more devoted to God and His purposes?) Remember that *specific* applications answer the questions who?, what?, when?, where?, and how?.

## Digging Deeper

1. Explain *how* reflecting God's righteousness and being used by Him as a peacemaker glorifies God and deepens our joy in our relationship with Him. Consult your Bible concordance and other reliable resources to help you formulate an answer. If you are a relatively new believer, you also may want to work on this question with a more mature Christian.

*"For those who would learn God's ways,
humility is the first thing,
humility is the second,
and humility is the third."*

∞

Aurelius Augustine

# Chapter Two

# *Genuine Wisdom Is Humble*

---

*What is the source of quarrels and conflicts among you? Is not the source your pleasures that wage war in your members? You lust and do not have; so you commit murder. And you are envious and cannot obtain; so you fight and quarrel. You do not have because you do not ask. You ask and do not receive, because you ask with wrong motives, so that you may spend it on your pleasures. You adulteresses, do you not know that friendship with the world is hostility toward God? Therefore whoever wishes to be a friend of the world makes himself an enemy of God. Or do you think that the Scripture speaks to no purpose: "He jealously desires the Spirit which He has made to dwell in us"? But He gives a greater grace. Therefore it says, "God is opposed to the proud, but gives grace to the humble." Submit therefore to God. Resist the devil and he will flee from you. Draw near to God and He will draw near to you. Cleanse your hands, you sinners; and purify your hearts, you double-minded. Be miserable and mourn and weep; let your laughter be turned into mourning, and your joy to gloom. Humble yourselves in the presence of the Lord, and He will exalt you. (James 4:1–10)*

When the Apostle Paul wrote his inspired letter to the believers in Philippi, he admonished them to be humble in their relationships with each other. He knew that God's pure genuine wisdom could not be understood and lived out by proud, arrogant people. Only those who are humble recognize their utter dependence upon the indwelling Spirit to learn and apply the revealed truths of God. They alone know that "earthen vessels" (2 Corinthians 4:7) are simply not strong enough "to live sensibly, righteously and godly in the present age" (Titus 2:12) without divine help. And they accede to genuine wisdom's demands that they keep their eyes fixed firmly on Christ and the pursuit of God's Kingdom.

Consider how Paul expressed this idea to the Philippians:

> *If therefore there is any encouragement in Christ, if there is any consolation of love, if there is any fellowship of the Spirit, if any affection and compassion, make my joy complete by being of the same mind, maintaining the same love, united in spirit, intent on one purpose. Do nothing from selfishness or empty conceit, but with humility of mind let each of you regard one another as more important than himself; do not merely look out for your own personal interests, but also for the interests of others. Have this attitude in yourselves which was also in Christ Jesus (2:1–5).*

Paul made similar entreaties in almost every letter he wrote. (For a few examples, see Romans 12:1–3; 1 Corinthians 1:10; Ephesians 4:1–3, Colossians 1:9–10, 3:1–2; and Titus 2:11–14.) He understood as well as James did that genuine wisdom's pure essence requires a heart of humility to make it effective.

Wisdom that is unstained by the world, the flesh, and the devil draws our attention to God and away from ourselves. It teaches us to fulfill our "chief end" by giving God glory in all that we do and by seeking full joy in our relationship with Him. It also unites us in heart, mind, and action with our siblings in Christ.

Whether we read James in the context of Paul, or Paul in the context of James, we find wisdom's heart of humility pumping the life of God's Spirit through the attitudes, actions, and thought patterns of wise believers. Those who are humble of mind, determined to love sacrificially, united in spirit, and intent on the one purpose for which they were saved will show forth the *effects* of God's pure wisdom: "peaceable, gentle, reasonable, full of mercy and good fruits, unwavering, without hypocrisy" (James 3:17).

James underscores humility's role in genuine wisdom by prefacing his practical illustrations with a clear warning against trading humble submission to Christ and God's purposes for a proud, arrogant focus on ourselves and the world.

### Wrong Motives

Christians who use Scripture to counsel troubled brothers and sisters know that at the root of most (if not all) unrighteous behavior lies a focus on self and/or the world instead of on God. James surely became an experienced and capable "biblical counselor" during his tenure as leader of the church in Jerusalem.

"What is the source of quarrels and conflicts among you?" he asks and then offers this keen diagnosis: "Is not the source your pleasures that wage war in your members?" (James 4:1). Did you notice that James wasn't as concerned with the quarrels and conflicts themselves as he was with their origin?

Believers in Christ frequently disagree with each other. When we do, we tend to concentrate *on the disagreement itself* by seeking to determine who's right and who's wrong. Although that effort may prove very valuable (especially for those who affirm Scripture's inerrant authority), the disagreement itself may not be the real issue. When disagreements escalate into "quarrels and conflicts," they become symptomatic of a much deeper problem. As James so aptly stated, they reflect an unrighteous self-centered focus on our "pleasures that wage war in [our] members"—in other words, a lack of humility.

Most of us find it remarkably easy to overlook this deeper problem in the heat of an argument, but wise gifted teachers down through the ages have cautioned us not to do so. In Psalm 8, David captured the soul of humility in his eloquent depiction of our complete dependence upon our Creator. Because we are by nature dependent beings, self-absorption is always counterproductive to God's purposes for us. That's why the prophet Isaiah reminds us that God dwells with "the contrite and lowly of spirit" (57:15), and Micah records God's requirement that we walk humbly with Him (6:8). Paul sums up humility well when he tells us to boast in the Lord (1 Corinthians 10:31; 2 Corinthians 10:17), not in ourselves (1 Corinthians 1:26–29) or in other people (3:18–21).

John Chrysostom, an early Church father, identified humility as "the foundation of our philosophy." Augustine said it was the first, second and third precept of the Christian religion. Thomas à Kempis and Bernard declared that the imitation of Christ is impossible without it. And Martin Luther warned against one of pride's cleverest disguises—"seeking to excel in humility"—when he said, "Unless a man is always humble, distrustful of himself, always fears his own understanding . . . passions . . . will, he will be unable to stand for long without offense. Truth will pass him by."[1]

John Calvin, characteristically, identified humility as a necessary means of exalting God's sovereignty. "Our humility is His loftiness," he said. Without it, we cannot practice self-denial  nor lay aside self-confidence and self-will in recognition of our dependence upon Him for everything.[2]

These men understood that we must be humble before we can apply the wisdom of God in our lives. When we focus on ourselves and the world, we are not intent upon God and the pursuit of His kingdom. Such pride constitutes spiritual adultery (James 4:4) because it transfers to illegitimate objects the committed devotion we owe to God alone. Spiritual adultery can't be hidden for long; it inevitably bears fruit that testifies of its lineage.

The first fruits of pride are usually born in our relationships with each other. The "unity of the Spirit," which we are instructed to "preserve . . . in the bond of peace" (Ephesians 4:3) is easily shattered by quarrels and conflicts. James says, "You lust and do not have; so you commit murder. And you are envious and cannot obtain; so you fight and quarrel" (v. 2). Preoccupation with self-seeking desire (lust) and self-exalting activities (envy) unleashes a destructive barrage of interpersonal sins, ranging from quarreling to murder, that devastate our unified witness. When that witness shatters, so does our ability to glorify God and enjoy Him intensely.

James indicates that spiritual adultery also bears bitter fruit in our relationship with our Father because of its harmful impact upon our prayers. Those who pray best are the most humble. They approach God's throne in awe of His sovereign majesty. They recognize their dependence upon Him for every aspect of being and acknowledge their gratitude for His mercy and grace. They affirm His exclusive right to their devotion, ask His forgiveness for their sins against Him, and claim His promises to meet all their needs in His service. (See Matthew 6:9–13.) Such humble prayers glorify God (John 14:13–15) and fill up our joy (John 16:24) because they focus our attention on Him instead of on ourselves. God-focused Christians pray very well (1 John 5:13–15); tragically, self-focused Christians do not.

When God's children lose sight of their dependence upon Him, they may simply stop praying. And as their sinful self-confidence quenches their prayers, it also slams shut the door on God's storehouse of blessing. James says these Christians don't have because they don't ask (James 4:2). When God's children retain a sense of their dependence on Him but couple it with consuming worldly desires, they may begin to view God as their "source" of earthly bliss. These Christians invariably continue to pray, but "with wrong motives" to "spend it on [their] pleasures." For that reason, James explains, when they ask, they will not receive (4:3).

Lack of humility is serious business. It negates both the understanding and practice of genuine wisdom. It has that effect because it is spiritual adultery as well as "friendship with the world,"—and "whoever wishes to be a friend of the world makes himself an enemy of God" (4:4).

Those who love God (as you and I do!) do not desire to make themselves His enemies. Thus, we want to be humble. However we have been warned that "pursuing humility" can be counterproductive. As Martin Luther has indicated, as soon as we say to ourselves *I believe I am humble,* we have fallen into pride's snare. So how can we "humble ourselves" as the Bible commands? It seems clear to me that we can't. Our only recourse is to throw ourselves on God's mercy and to rely on His "greater grace."

### Greater Grace

Grace cannot be received by someone who is proud. That's because grace, by definition, is *"unmerited favor,"* and the proud person believes that the favor is *merited.* God's gift of grace is reserved for the humble because they alone know that they don't deserve it.

Most of us think of grace as being received at the time of salvation (Ephesians 2:8–9; Titus 3:4–7), but we tend to forget that it doesn't stop there. And such forgetfulness is not very wise. If we are to live sensibly in the present age, we must remember the equipping effects of the grace of salvation. As God's saving grace places us in His family, it transforms and sustains us to live out the purpose for which He redeemed us.[3]

If we bear that truth in mind, we won't fall prey to the counterfeit wisdom that misdefines grace as the freedom to live "however we choose." D. Edmond Hiebert, in his commentary on James, emphasizes that God's promise of grace was never intended to encourage His people to think lightly of sin.[4] Our Father is jealous of our devotion (James 4:5)[5] and demands from us wholehearted loyalty (2 Corinthians 5:14–15). Sin draws our attention from Him to ourselves while it splits our allegiance between His pursuits and the world's. Therefore, the grace that He gives us cannot be rightly seen as a license to sin. Rather, as one of my favorite Bible teachers has said, "Grace does not mean that we have permission to do as we please; it means we have the power to do what pleases God."

Paul dealt with this issue decisively in his epistle to the Christians in Rome. Although "where sin increased, grace abounded all the more" (Romans 5:20), we are *not* (definitely, emphatically not) "to continue in sin that grace might increase" (6:1–2). That's because we have died to sin (v. 2) and have been united with Christ (v. 5). God's saving grace has freed us from sin's power (vv. 6, 14), has enslaved us to God (v. 22), and sustains us as we pursue righteousness (vv. 12–13) by obeying God from the heart (v. 17).

The transforming grace that enables us to live out God's purpose for our salvation is what James calls "greater grace." It is grace that does more than confirm our reservations in heaven. It is the grace that we find at God's merciful throne when we look to His help in our time of need (Hebrews 4:16). It is the grace that convicts us by the work of the Spirit when we succumb to the allure of the world, the flesh, and the devil—then draws us to confess and seek His cleansing forgiveness. It is the grace that removes our transgressions from us "as far as the east is from the west" (Psalm 103:12–13) and gives us innumerable chances to start over again (1 John 1:9). And it is the grace that teaches us how to live for God's glory in inexpressible joy (Psalm 32:8–11).

### Humble Yourselves

Thomas Manton likened knowing sound doctrine to drawing a bow—and applying that knowledge to hitting the target. He then went on to comment that many Christians are "wise" in the generalities of doctrine, but foolish in actual practice.[6] James doesn't want his beloved readers to be included in Manton's description. Therefore he extends his discussion of humility beyond knowing doctrine to applying it in our lives.

"Don't be foolishly satisfied with the mere knowledge of what humility is," he says in effect. "Be truly wise by putting that knowledge to work—by humbling yourselves." James emphasizes five aspects of *humbling ourselves*: (1) submission to God, (2) resisting the devil, (3) drawing near to God, (4) repenting of sin, and (5) trusting God. Did you notice that three of the five fix our attention directly on God while the other two must be done in reference to Him? That coincides perfectly with the doctrinal teaching of Scripture regarding the practice of humility: It rests upon understanding our utter dependence on God. James now urges us to live wisely by acting in ways that reflect that understanding.

Humbling ourselves requires, first of all, an *attitude* of submission to God. An attitude is a settled opinion or way of thinking. Attitudes develop over time as a result of thoughtfully considering the realities of life. They are more mental than emotional and more persistent than temporary. I like to think of them as the "colored glasses" through which we view life.

An attitude of submission acknowledges and yields willingly to rightful authority. Submissive Christians delight to work under God instead of against Him. They are not after God's job because they know they can't do it. They rejoice in the security they find in His sovereignty and appreciate being chosen to participate in His work. They know that they are creatures dependent on their Creator for every facet of life. If we are among them, we have the mindset we need to practice humility.

This attitude of submission must completely encompass the four actions we take to "humble ourselves"— resisting the devil, drawing near to God, repenting of sin, and trusting our Father. We must recognize our fallen inability to do any of these without the equipping power of His Holy Spirit.

Effectively resisting Satan certainly demands complete dependence on God. Peter describes Satan as a "roaring lion" who prowls about "seeking someone to devour" (1 Peter 5:8). But he also affirms that Satan is no match for the Christian who is submitted to God. "But resist him, firm in your faith," Peter says (v. 9), *after* you have "[cast] all your anxiety upon Him, because He cares for you" (v. 7) and *knowing* that "the God of all grace . . . will Himself perfect, confirm, strengthen and establish you" (v. 10).

What a comfort to know that we don't have to face Satan alone, and how foolish we are when we try to do so!

Wisdom dictates that we follow the archangel Michael's example. Jude tells us "when he [Michael] disputed with the devil and argued about the body of Moses, [he] did not dare pronounce against him a railing judgment, but said, 'The Lord rebuke you'" (v. 9). An attitude of submission reminds us of our childlike reliance upon the Mighty One who created Satan, allowed him to fall, and defeated him soundly at Calvary (John 12:30–33).

That same attitude also enables us to draw near to God. Scripture tells us that God is "near to the broken-hearted" (Psalm 34:18), will not despise "a broken and contrite spirit" (51:17). And that although heaven is His throne and the earth His footstool, He will look to "him who is humble and contrite of spirit, and who trembles at [His] word" (Isaiah 66:1–2).

Without a submissive spirit, our fallen propensity for self-justification will interfere with repentance of our sin. We must depend upon God, who is supremely able and willing to search our hearts, reveal our sin to us, and help us confess it (Psalm 19:12–14; 139:23–24; 1 Corinthians 4:3–4).

Finally, an attitude of submission encourages us to trust God. Inherent dependence walks hand in hand with necessary reliance. And when the One to whom we must look for protection and care is all–powerful, righteous, and good, we quickly learn to trust Him completely. Thus, James's command, "Humble yourselves in the presence of the Lord" (James 4:10), is not an ominous threat but a thrilling privilege. Submission has taught us that God keeps His promises; therefore, we know (definitely, emphatically *know*) that He will exalt us.

1   The information in this paragraph, as well as the quotation from
    Martin Luther, was cited in R. E. O. White, "Humility," in *Evangelical
    Dictionary of Theology*, ed. Walter A. Elwell (Grand Rapids: Baker
    Book House, 1984), 537.

2   John T. McNeill, editor, *The Library of Christian Classics*, Volumes XX
    and XXI—*Calvin: Institutes of the Christian Religion*, translated by Ford
    Lewis Battles (Philadelphia: The Westminster Press, 1960), II. ii. 11;
    III. vii. 4, xii. 6–7.

3   For a most helpful discussion of this important truth, see Jerry
    Bridges, *Transforming Grace: Living Confidently In God's Unfailing Love*.
    Colorado Springs: NavPress, 1991.

4   D. Edmond Hiebert, *James* (Chicago: Moody Press, 1979, 1992), 235.

5   This verse is another "interpretive nightmare" which has generated
    much lively discussion among commentators on James. It seems
    fairly obvious from the context that aside from the questions that the
    verse raises, the verse does indicate that God expects and requires
    exclusive devotion and loyalty from His children.

6   Thomas Manton, *The Crossway Classic Commentaries: James*, series edi-
    tors Alister McGrath and J. I. Packer (Wheaton, Ill.: Crossway Books,
    1995), 245.

# Review Questions

1. Read Romans 12:1–16; Ephesians 4:1–16; Philippians 2:1–13; Colossians 1:9–14; 3:1–2; and Titus 2:11–14. Then reread James 3:13–4:10. Use the truths of God found in these verses to help you explain why genuine wisdom (which is essentially *pure* because it is from God) requires a *heart of humility* to make it effective.

2. Describe the "deeper problem" that was producing quarrels and conflicts among James's readers. Give several examples of cautions that wise and gifted teachers, down through the ages, have given against overlooking this problem when we disagree with each other. Then explain why we would be wise to heed their advice.

3. Describe the "fruit" born by prideful self-absorption (which James equates with spiritual adultery) both in our relationships with each other and in our relationship with our Father. How does this fruit influence the way we live out God's purpose for us?

4. Explain D. Edmond Hiebert's insightful, true statement that God's promise of grace was never intended to encourage his people to think lightly of sin. (Be sure to include a description of how God's grace does more than confirm our reservations in heaven.)

5. List and briefly describe the five aspects of "humbling ourselves" that James emphasizes in 4:7–10. Explain the relationship between the first aspect he mentions, which is an attitude, to the other four, which are actions.

---

6. Look up *humility* and/or *humble* in a biblical dictionary, or consult reliable commentaries on James 4:1–10 regarding these words. Based upon what you have learned from those sources and from this lesson, write a definition of *humility* in your own words. Then explain why humility is a necessary ingredient in wise Christian living.

## Applying the Word

1. Describe your last disagreement with another Christian. How did you handle the situation? Describe your attitudes, thoughts, and actions as well as the actions of the other believer. (You cannot describe his or her attitudes and thoughts accurately, of course.) Did the disagreement escalate into a quarrel or a conflict? If so, describe the circumstances surrounding the escalation. Was the disagreement resolved? If so, how? Considering what you have learned in this lesson, do you believe that a lack of humility *on your part* may have played a role in the disagreement itself or its escalation into a quarrel or conflict? If so, what specific changes do you need to make in your attitudes, thoughts, and actions that will help you handle future disagreements with other Christians in ways that will glorify God and increase your joy in your relationship with Him?

2. Let's not be foolishly satisfied with a mere knowledge of what humility is. Let's be truly wise by putting that knowledge to work by humbling ourselves! Answer the following questions honestly and specifically.

Are there areas of your life in which you are resisting (or actively rebelling against) God's rightful authority over you? If so, describe the areas and your attitude. What steps must you take to develop an attitude of submission to God in these areas? Make a specific plan to help you develop this attitude.

Do you believe that Satan is currently "seeking to devour you" in some particular way? If so, how can you benefit from the example of the archangel Michael in Jude 9 as you work at resisting him?

Are some of your current activities preventing you from drawing near to God? If so, with what specific activities will you replace them?

Are you harboring unconfessed sin? If so, use Psalm 19:12–14, Psalm 139:23–24, and 1 John 1:9 to help you seek God's cleansing forgiveness immediately.

When was the last time you meditated on God's power, righteousness, and goodness as a means of strengthening your trust in Him? If it has been more than a week, use a concordance to locate Scripture passages describing these attributes of God; then devote an hour or more to thoughtful consideration of how these aspects of His nature encourage submission and trust on your part.

# Digging Deeper

1. Explain why grace is not "permission to do as we please" but, rather, "having the power to do what pleases God." Support your explanation with Scripture.

2. Relate James's description of the effects of God's wisdom (3:17) with the aspects of humbling ourselves that he outlines in 4:7–10 by answering the following questions:

   How does an attitude of submission foster the wise *attitudes* of peaceableness, gentleness, and reasonableness?

How does resisting Satan, drawing near to God, repenting of sin, and trusting God generate wise actions that are full of mercy and good fruits?

How do these four activities stimulate wise *thinking* that is characterized less and less by hypocrisy and more and more by unwavering devotion to God and His purposes?

*"To believe actively that our heavenly Father
constantly spreads around us
the providential circumstances
that work for our present good
and our everlasting well-being,
brings to the soul a veritable benediction....
Our insistence on seeing ahead is natural enough,
but it is a real hindrance to our spiritual progress.
God has charged Himself with full responsibility
for our eternal happiness
and stands ready to take over the
management of our lives
the moment we turn in faith to Him."*

A.W. Tozer

# Chapter Three

## *Genuine Wisdom Submits to God*

---

*Do not speak against one another, brethren. He who speaks against a brother, or judges his brother, speaks against the law, and judges the law; but if you judge the law, you are not a doer of the law, but a judge of it. There is only one Lawgiver and Judge, the One who is able to save and to destroy; but who are you who judge your neighbor? Come now, you who say, "Today or tomorrow, we shall go to such and such a city, and spend a year there and engage in business and make a profit." Yet you do not know what your life will be like tomorrow. You are just a vapor that appears for a little while and then vanishes away. Instead, you ought to say, "If the Lord wills, we shall live and also do this or that." But as it is, you boast in your arrogance; all such boasting is evil. Therefore, to one who knows the right thing to do, and does not do it, to him it is sin. (James 4:11–17)*

All of us seem to have a built-in aversion to the idea of submission. Just mention the word in a room full of women and you'll see what I mean! But we ladies haven't cornered the market on that reaction. Don't you know a few men who would rather spend six hours lost than ask for directions? How many times has a toddler (male or female) looked you right in the eye while proceeding to do exactly what you had forbidden? Don't most of us (men and women alike) drive five miles over the speed limit as a matter of habit? Didn't we persistently come home ten minutes past curfew when we were teenagers?

Aversion to submission isn't gender specific. Rather it is specific to our fallen sin nature. The Westminster Shorter Catechism defines *sin* as "any want of conformity unto, or transgression of, the law of God" (Q/A 14). In practical terms, we could boil that down to "submission aversion." Sins of omission (want of conformity unto the law of God) and sins of commission (transgression of the law of God) reflect an attitude of defiance against rightful authority, which is rooted in pride.

James tells us that such an attitude is extremely unwise. Rightful authority, in all of its forms, has been instituted by God for His own glory and, consequently, for the good of His people. God created us as dependent beings subject to authority because that condition enhances His glory and fills up our joy. Pastor-teacher John Piper expressed it like this: "All the omnipotent energy that drives the heart of God to pursue His own glory, also drives Him to satisfy the hearts of those who seek their joy in Him."[1]

Satan roots sin in pride to disrupt both of those purposes. He knows, from personal experience (Isaiah 14:12–17), that creatures absorbed with themselves do not seek to fulfill God's purposes for them. He delights in luring God's children away from pursuit of the Kingdom with provocative calls to arrogant self-reliance.

In Chapter Two, we saw how James exhorted his readers to wisely acknowledge their dependence on God, humble themselves in His presence, and expect opposition from Satan (James 4:1–10). In this chapter, we will concentrate on his description of three practical areas in which we must apply that exhortation (vv. 11–17). As Christians, we must practice submission to God in (1) the ways in which we speak about and to others, (2) the ways in which we plan our activities, and (3) the ways in which we respond to God's truth in general.

### Critical Speech Judges God's Law

James has already exhorted his readers at length regarding the importance of controlling their tongues (3:1–12). Thus at this point in his discussion of wisdom, he simply reminds us that our speech indicates the state of our hearts. A proud, arrogant spirit finds it remarkably easy to "speak against" others (v. 11). It expresses itself in biting criticism, scathing condemnation, and careless gossip. It does not hesitate to falsely accuse, exaggerate faults, malign motives, rehash mistakes, and assassinate character. It gives no thought to the edification of others because its attention is focused fully on itself. Those who hold lofty views of themselves must, of necessity, look down on others. And no one should be surprised when they speak accordingly.

Psalm 101:5 associates slander with a haughty look and an arrogant heart. It also affirms that God *will not endure* those who are characterized by such behavior and attitudes. James doesn't pull any punches when he explains God's intransigence: "He who speaks against a brother, or judges his brother, speaks against the law, and judges the law; but if you judge the law, you are not a doer of the law, but a judge of it. There is only one Lawgiver and Judge, the One who is able to save and to destroy; but who are you to judge your neighbor?" (vv. 11–12).

Early in his letter, James admonished his readers to be doers of God's law and not merely hearers (1:22). At that point he was emphasizing our need to practice God's truth to overcome trials, but now he proceeds to broaden that emphasis. Doing God's law "works" well in trials because it is the key to wise living in general.

God did not give us His law in the language of suggestion. Nowhere in Scripture does He ask our opinion of His commandments. Since God alone has full, perfect knowledge of His plans and purposes, He does not give us the right to pass judgment on His proclamations. When we read God's law and *decide* not to obey it, we usurp a prerogative God has reserved for Himself. We arrogantly assert our fallen opinion that a particular law is not worth obeying. We exalt ourselves above God, discard the "wisdom from above" (James 3:17) in favor of that which is "earthly, natural, demonic" (v. 15), and clear the way for jealousy, selfish ambition, disorder, and every evil thing to disrupt God's family (v. 16).

Naturally, exchanging God's truth for the ways of the world profoundly affects the ways in which we speak about and to others. When our attitudes are so arrogant as to judge God and His law, we will think nothing of judging our brothers and sisters as well. The Greek word translated *judge* in verse 11 (*krino*) means "to sit in judgment" or "to pass judgment," and carries the idea of condemnation.[2] It describes another activity that God has wisely and rightly reserved for Himself. We fallen humans are simply not qualified to judge others because we lack full knowledge and perfect integrity.

God's law commands us to love each other instead. James had undoubtedly heard his brother Jesus declare that "the whole Law and the Prophets" depend upon these two commandments: "You shall love the Lord your God with all your heart, and with all your soul, and with all your mind . . . [and] love your neighbor as yourself" (Matthew 22:37–39). James surely understood that those who love God will not worship other gods, make graven images, take His Name in vain, nor profane His Sabbath—and that those who love their neighbors will not murder them, lie to them, steal from them, commit adultery against them, covet their possessions, nor dishonor their closest neighbors, their parents. (See Exodus 20:1–17.)

That is why James told his readers to govern their human relationships by God's "royal law" (2:8). When we do that, we will not speak *against* others but rather for the purpose of edification (Ephesians 4:29). Speech that edifies others does not condemn them. Rather it calls them to pursue their highest interests by submitting themselves to God's commandments.

Many Christians misunderstand the nature and purpose of edification, thinking that it must always be pleasant and easy to hear. But, realistically, that is simply not true. Words that edify not only compliment and commend those who do well, but they also gently rebuke and exhort those who commit sin or fail to walk worthy of their high calling in Christ. Thus, those who interpret "Do not judge your brother" to mean "Never reprove or correct" are just as unloving as those who condemn. Paul, in his classic definition of love, tells us that it "does not rejoice in unrighteousness, but rejoices with the truth" (1 Corinthians 13:6). Paul knew that evaluating the behavior of others in light of God's truth and restoring those "caught in any trespass . . . *in a spirit of gentleness*" (Galatians 6:1; italics added for emphasis) is not condemnation, but edification motivated by love.

Wise Christians submit to the "one Lawgiver and Judge" in their interactions with others. They acknowledge His sovereign right to judge His creatures' behavior, and they accept His standard of Scripture as the sole criteria for the edification of others. These wise Christians aren't hard to recognize: Their manner of speech reflects the state of their hearts.

### Independence in Planning Is Practical Atheism

William Ernest Henley has eloquently captured the meaning of the phrase *practical atheism* in his famous poem "Invictus."[3]

> *Out of the night that covers me,*
> *Black as the Pit from pole to pole*
> *I thank whatever gods may be*
> *For my unconquerable soul.*

> *In the fell clutch of circumstance*
> *I have not winced nor cried aloud.*
> *Under the bludgeonings of chance*
> *My head is bloody, but unbowed.*

> *Beyond this place of wrath and tears*
> *Looms by the Horror of the shade,*

*And yet the menace of the years*
*Finds, and shall find me unafraid.*

*It matters not how strait the gate,*
*How charged with punishments the scroll,*
*I am the master of my fate;*
*I am the captain of my soul.*

Simon J. Kistemaker describes practical atheism much more succinctly as living as if God does not exist. And then he goes on to say that practical atheism is one of *the most common sins committed by Christians.*[4] Does that statement surprise you—perhaps even shock you? If so, you were probably jarred by the use of the word *"atheism"* in regard to a believer. It definitely caught your attention! Maybe it even forced you to stop and think. Could that be why so many good teachers use the phrase *practical atheism* to depict James's warning to the independently minded?

"Come now," James says to his readers, "you who say, 'Today or tomorrow, we shall go to such and such a city, and spend a year there and engage in business and make a profit.' Yet you do not know what your life will be like tomorrow. You are just a vapor that appears for a little while and then vanishes away. Instead you ought to say, 'If the Lord wills, we shall live and also do this or that'" (4:13–15).

Was James anti-business? or anti–profit? or anti–diligence? No, he was not. We must interpret his words in the context in which he was writing. James wants his readers to live *wisely* as Christians. He knows we can't do that by pursuing our daily activities as if God doesn't exist. Such arrogance is unwise because it fails to glorify God and fill up our joy. John Blanchard, in his book *Truth for Life*, explains it this way: "Now of course James was not suggesting that they just sit back and do nothing. He was not condemning their business but their boasting; not their industry but their independence; not their acumen but their arrogance. What he is telling them is that the right attitude to life is to recognize that God is in sovereign control of it all, and that it should be yielded in humble submission to his divine will."[5]

Wise Christians do more than pay lip service to God's absolute sovereignty; they order their lives in complete dependence upon it. When they close their Bibles to go do their chores, they don't forget that God alone gives "life and breath" to all things (Acts 17:25). They face each new day's assortment of joys, troubles, and challenges secure in the knowledge that He is the reason they "live and move and exist" (Acts17: 28). They lean on His Spirit for guidance in all their endeavors and delight to be used as His means to accomplish His purposes. They work hard by day and sleep well by night because they have learned to rely completely on God's all-sufficient grace, which is abundant for every good deed (2 Corinthians 9:8). They do not use God's sovereign provision as a justification for sloth or for lack of planning. Rather, in the paraphrased words of D. Edmond Hiebert, they commit all to Him and continue according to plan "under the encouraging sense of God's guidance and sustaining grace."[6]

Wise Christians are those who have rightly chosen to walk humbly with God instead of to walk proudly without Him (Deuteronomy 10:12–13; Micah 6:8). They glorify God by their acknowledged dependence upon Him and fill up their joy in their unfailing confidence in His perfect care. Their lives reveal the reality of the faith at work in them.

## Knowing Without Doing Is Sin

James skillfully summarizes the wisdom of submission when he says to his readers, "But as it is, you boast in your arrogance; all such boasting is evil. Therefore, to one who knows the right thing to do, and does not do it, to him it is sin" (4:16–17). His words serve to remind us again that every sin in the book is rooted in pride.

Whenever we yield to the temptation to think more highly of ourselves than we ought, submission to God slips inexorably toward arrogant independence. When we allow ourselves to lose sight of our utter dependence on God, our allegiance soon shifts from pursuit of His Kingdom to self-exaltation.

We may be running well—focused on God, taking every thought captive to Christ, seeking the Spirit's enablement to serve Him effectively, and expressing our gratitude for successes in ministry. Our confidence builds, and our guard drops a little. We forget the wise words of our brother Paul, "Therefore let him who thinks he stands take heed lest he fall" (1 Corinthians 10:12), and open a chink in our spiritual armor. Satan, our vigilant enemy, quickly attacks at the vulnerable spot by slyly complimenting our personal achievements, to which we are apt to respond, *Why, thank you. I did do rather well in that ministry effort, didn't I?* Thus begins our destructive descent of the slippery slope of "arrogant independence."

As our slide gains momentum, we make easier targets. Satan does not have to work nearly so hard to keep us rolling downhill once we've started moving. That's why every Christian should memorize Paul's warning in 1 Corinthians 10:12 along with his words of encouragement in the verse that follows: "No temptation has overtaken you but such as is common to man; and God is faithful, who will not allow you to be tempted beyond what you are able, but with the temptation will provide the way of escape also, that you may be able to endure it."

Wise Christians know that their best defense against the temptations of the world, the flesh, and the devil is to maintain a good grip on the truth of God's Word. If we consistently learn it and do it, we will not slip so often. And when we do drop our guard and find ourselves falling, we can use God's Word, stored in our hearts, as an emergency handhold. All we need do to arrest our descent is reach out and grasp a well-placed memory verse.

Since our enemy knows that our deadliest weapon against him is Scripture, he works hard to drive wedges between it and us. If we want to live wisely in the present age, we must rely on God's truth as our means of *recognizing* (taking heed lest we fall) and *defeating* (laying hold of God's way of escape) the temptation of pride—particularly when it comes as an assault on the Bible itself.

When Satan appeals to our intellect by insisting that Scripture has no inherent authority, is unreliable, and hardly sufficient for "New Millennium" Christians, we must recall that he is the father of lies, who delights in discrediting truth (John 8:44–45). When he flatters us by suggesting that we are fully capable of running our lives without the "crutch" of a dusty old book, we must remember the heartbreaking examples of others he has deceived down through the ages. (See Genesis 3:1–5 and 2 Samuel 11–12 for two clear examples.) When he assures us that we are thoroughly qualified to pass judgment on Scripture by accepting some passages and discarding others, we must follow Christ's example of righteous humility and respond that our lives depend upon *"every word* that proceeds out of the mouth of God" (Matthew 4:4; italics added for emphasis).

Satan's assaults on God's Word are carefully calculated to separate our behavior from what we know from Scripture is "the right thing to do" (James 4:17). He does that by appealing to our built-in aversion to being submissive. Every time he persuades us to *judge* Scripture instead of *obey* it, he persuades us to sin. And when we sin, we cease to pursue our chief end as God's children. We then must repent and confess to get back on track (1 John 1:9).

Christians do not have to succumb to Satan's devices. God gives us everything that we need for life and godliness (2 Peter 1:3–4) in His Word and His Spirit (Ephesians 5:18ff; Colossians 3:16ff). We *have been equipped* to glorify God and enjoy Him forever by living sensibly, righteously, and godly in the present age. But using that equipment effectively requires our complete dependence on Him. Humble submission to God is thus the key to wise living—which, by the way, also opens the door to the *righteous* exaltation that God Himself has prepared for us (James 4:10; 1 Peter 5:6).

[1] John Piper, *Desiring God: Meditations of a Christian Hedonist* (Sisters, Ore.: Multnomah Books, 1986, 1996), 53.

[2] W. E. Vine, Merrill F. Unger, and William White Jr., *Vine's Expository Dictionary of Biblical Words,* s.v. "Judge" (Nashville, Tenn.: Thomas Nelson Publishers, 1985).

[3] Quoted in John MacArthur Jr., *The MacArthur New Testament Commentary: James* (Chicago: Moody Press, 1998), 234.

[4] Simon J. Kistemaker, *New Testament Commentary: Exposition of James, Epistles of John, Peter, and Jude* (Grand Rapids: Baker Books, 1996), 146. Originally published in separate volumes.

[5] John Blanchard, *Truth For Life: A Devotional Commentary on the Epistle of James* (Durham, England: Evangelical Press, 1986), 315.

[6] D. Edmond Hiebert, *James* (Chicago: Moody Press, 1979, 1992), 254.

# Review Questions

1. Practically speaking, how does the Westminster Shorter Catechism's definition of sin boil down to "submission aversion"? Read James 4:1–17 in the light of Proverbs 3:1–25, Isaiah 14:12–16, Romans 8:31–39, and 1 Peter 5:6–11; then use what you learn from your reading to explain why submission aversion is extremely unwise.

2. List the three *practical areas* James describes in which we must apply his exhortations in 4:1–10 to acknowledge our dependence on God, humble ourselves in His presence, and expect opposition from Satan. Do you think that James has "covered the bases" of Christian submission by using these particular examples? In other words, can you think of any areas of Christian submission that are not covered by his discussion of these three areas?

3. Describe several ways in which a proud, arrogant spirit can be revealed in our speech. What does Psalm 101:5 say about those with proud, arrogant spirits? What light does James shed on God's attitude toward the arrogant in 4:11–12?

4. What effect does exchanging God's truth for the ways of the world have upon the ways in which we speak about and to others? What effect does obeying God's command to love each other have upon our speech? (In your answer, be sure to explain the difference between condemnation and edification.)

5. What is "practical atheism"? Can you think of some ways in which you have been (or are) guilty of committing this sin? How should we guard against committing this sin?

6. How will memorizing 1 Corinthians 10:12–13 help us avoid or climb back up the slippery slope of arrogant independence? If you have not already done so, begin memorizing these verses this week.

7. Describe the purpose behind Satan's attempts to separate us
   from Scripture. How does humble submission to God help us
   resist his attacks on God's Word?

## Applying the Word

1. For a period of one or two days, carry a small notebook (or a tape recorder) and record as many samples of your own speech as possible. Then review those samples prayerfully. Ask the Holy Spirit to search your heart in regard to your speech (Psalm 139:23–24). Does your speech reveal an arrogant, condemning attitude toward others, or a heart given to gentle edification? Cite specific examples to support your conclusion.

Describe your daily routine during a typical week. Be brief but thorough. Then prayerfully consider your typical attitude while pursuing your normal activities. Are you constantly aware of God's sovereign control of your circumstances? Do you frequently think or speak short prayers of gratitude, adoration, confession, and intercession appropriate to various situations? Do particular passages of Scripture come to mind as you react to people and events? Are you acutely aware of God's gracious enablement as you carry out your responsibilities? Evaluate the answers to these questions and determine whether you are behaving as a practical atheist or as a submissive believer.

Meditate on 1 Corinthians 10:12–13 and ask the Lord to make you aware of Satan's specific attempts to drive wedges between you and His Word. Are you tempted to doubt its authority, reliability, or sufficiency? Do you sometimes think that it is irrelevant as a guide for daily living or that you are free to pick and choose among its instructions? Have you sinned by behaving contrary to what you know to be right? If so, cite specific examples.

Complete this application exercise by confessing any and all sin that it has revealed and by praying in accordance with Psalm 19:12–14.

---

2. Choose some creative way to illustrate the idea that *humble submission to God is the key to wise living*. Write a short story or poem, compose a song, perform a skit, or draw a picture or diagram. How could you use your illustration in ministry? Make plans to follow through by putting your illustration to use in some particular way.

# Digging Deeper

1. Relate the all-encompassing nature of James's three practical examples in 4:11–17 (see Review Question 2) to the concept of Scripture's reliability and sufficiency.

2. Explain the relationship between God's Law as summarized in the Ten Commandments, Jesus' words in Matthew 22:37–39, and Paul's exhortation to speak "only such a word as is good for edification" (Ephesians 4:29).

*"It is God's nature
to make something out of nothing,
that is why He cannot make anything
out of him
who is not yet nothing."*

Martin Luther

# Chapter Four

## *A Few Words for the Fools*

---

*Come now, you rich, weep and howl for your miseries which are coming upon you. Your riches have rotted and your garments have become moth-eaten. Your gold and your silver have rusted; and their rust will be a witness against you and will consume your flesh like fire. It is in the last days that you have stored up your treasure! Behold, the pay of the laborers who mowed your fields, and which has been withheld by you, cries out against you; and the outcry of those who did the harvesting has reached the ears of the Lord of Sabaoth. You have lived luxuriously on the earth and led a life of wanton pleasure; you have fattened your hearts in a day of slaughter. You have condemned and put to death the righteous man; he does not resist you. (James 5:1–6)*

In the Old Testament book of Proverbs, a wise man named Agur asked two things of God:

> *Keep deception and lies far from me,*
> *Give me neither poverty nor riches;*
> *Feed me with the food that is my portion,*
> *Lest I be full and deny Thee and say, "Who is the*
>     *Lord?"*
> *Or lest I be in want and steal,*
> *And profane the name of my God. (30:7–9)*

The wisdom of Agur is clearly revealed in his requests. He understood the value of truth; and he recognized the depravity of his own heart. By asking the Lord to "keep deception and lies far from [him]," he revealed his commitment to live by "every word that proceeds out of the mouth of God" (Matthew 4:4). And when he asked to be given neither riches nor poverty, he disclosed his sensitivity to his own weakness. He knew that riches would tempt him to arrogant independence, whereas poverty might persuade him to excuse sinful behavior. He also knew that walking down either path would dishonor God and short-circuit his own chief end of being.

Agur's words might remind you of those that James wrote in the early part of his letter: "But let the brother of humble circumstances glory in his high position; and let the rich man glory in his humiliation, because like flowering grass he will pass away. For the sun rises with a scorching wind, and withers the grass; and its flower falls off, and the beauty of its appearance is destroyed; so too the rich man in the midst of his pursuits will fade away" (1:9–11). Although phrased as an exhortation instead of a request, James's words also address the temptations inherent in extreme financial conditions.

James warns the poor man to "glory in his high position"—that is, to remember that straited circumstances do not justify sin. Those who have few earthly possessions must look to the Lord in their need and honor Him with their humble dependence. James then warns the rich man to "glory in his humiliation" by refusing to rely on wealth or position. Those who have been blessed with an abundance of worldly goods must acknowledge God as their source just as He is of salvation.[1]

In these verses James emphasizes the importance of depending on God in the midst of trials, and in 5:1–12 he expands on that theme. Dependence is an essential ingredient of submission to God—which, as we saw in the previous chapter, is the key to wise living.

James underscores this truth boldly in these twelve verses. He first launches a scathing attack on the ungodly rich. These people are not well-meaning believers, temporarily distracted from Christ by their worldly wealth and position. Rather they are those who reject God and His purposes in favor of greed. They spurn the biblical teaching that the world's goods come from God with two conditions attached: they are never to be the source of our hope, and they are to be generously shared with those in need (1 Timothy 6:17–19). In verses 1–6 of Chapter 5, James condemns the foolish rich for their self-indulgence and lack of compassion. He then comforts those whom the rich fools have abused by reminding them of the wisdom of patient endurance (vv. 7-12), which is also involved in submission to God. In this lesson we'll take a look at James's words to the fools; in our next, we'll concentrate on his words to the wise.

## The Madness of Materialism

In his tape series *Developing a Christian Mind*, James Montgomery Boice makes the profound (and downright startling) point that failure to think Christianly amounts to insanity. What a refreshing perspective that is in a society that characterizes radical Christians as ill-equipped for life in the "real world"! Boice condemns society's view as simply ridiculous. The truth is that those who persistently try to think outside of the context of God's absolute sovereignty are, in fact, out of touch with reality! [2]

Boice supports his assertion by taking us to the book of Daniel. There we read of Nebuchadnezzar, a powerful king who was driven insane because of his godless thinking. While walking on the roof of his royal palace one day, he reflected and said, "Is this not Babylon the great, which *I myself* have built as a royal residence by the might of *my* power and for the glory of *my* majesty?" (Daniel 4:29–30, italics added for emphasis ).

We would be hard pressed to find a better example of trying to think outside of the context of God's absolute sovereignty. And the next few verses describe the price that Nebuchadnezzar paid for such thinking: "[H]e was driven away from mankind and began eating grass like cattle, and his body was drenched with the dew of heaven, until his hair had grown like eagles' feathers and his nails like birds' claws" (vv. 31–33). One of the world's greatest rulers had become completely insane.

God required Nebuchadnezzar to reap what he had sown. Insane behavior invariably results from thinking without a God-centered perspective. The ungodly rich whom James addresses reflect the same truth. They too had divorced God from their patterns of thinking and were thus reaping a life controlled by what John Blanchard calls "the madness of materialism."[3]

These people personified arrogant independence. They had not an ounce of humility in them. Instead of submitting themselves to God's authority and perfect provision, they hoarded the wealth of the world and placed all their trust in it. Their worldly attitude toward money and material goods clearly revealed the state of their hearts. These people were not children of God because they worshipped mammon (Matthew 6:24).

James speaks to them in terms of condemnation, not only to warn them of impending judgment but also to encourage the hearts of those they were abusing. "[W]eep and howl," he commands them, "for your miseries which are coming upon you. Your riches have rotted and your garments have become moth-eaten. Your gold and your silver have rusted; and their rust will be a witness against you and will consume your flesh like fire. It is in the last days that you have stored up your treasure!" (5: 1–3).

These ungodly rich were tragically out of touch with reality. Because they had refused to acknowledge God as the source of all good things (James 1:17), they would eventually see those good things disintegrate. Because they selfishly had spurned God's purpose for wealth (1 John 3:17–18), they would soon hear their tarnished riches bear witness against them. Stored-up worldly treasure would do them no good when they stood before the Judge of the Universe to give an account of their lives (Matthew 6:19–21). They had made the deadly mistake of allowing their riches to possess them instead of possessing their riches to the glory of God.

John Blanchard says that the only cure for the madness of materialism is the sanity of stewardship.[4] The ungodly rich are doomed to destruction unless they return to their senses—as did Nebuchadnezzar. In the book of Daniel, he tells us what happened: "But at the end of that period [of insanity] I, Nebuchadnezzar, raised my eyes toward heaven, and my reason returned to me, and I blessed the Most High and praised and honored Him who lives forever;

*For His dominion is an everlasting dominion,*
*And His kingdom endures from generation to*
*generation.*
*And all the inhabitants of the earth are accounted as*
*nothing.*
*But He does according to His will in the host of heaven*
*And among the inhabitants of earth;*
*And no one can ward off His hand*
*Or say to Him, 'What hast Thou done?'*

"At that time my reason returned to me. And . . . I was reestablished in my sovereignty, and surpassing greatness was added to me. Now I Nebuchadnezzar praise, exalt, and honor the King of heaven, for all His works are true and His ways just, and He is able to humble those who walk in pride" (4:34–37).

Nebuchadnezzar was, at long last, equipped for life in the real world—the world as it actually is—governed by God. Unfortunately, James gives us no indication that the ungodly rich to whom he was speaking ever learned that wise lesson.

### Greed Breeds Indulgence and Strangles Compassion

Contrary to what some people believe, there is nothing intrinsically evil in wealth, nor is there any inherent value in poverty. Many of God's most faithful saints have been rich, and just as many (or more) of the world's greatest sinners have been poverty-stricken.

Both conditions of life carry their own peculiar blessings and curses. The rich have the resources (and usually the ability and influence) to accomplish a great deal in ministry, whereas the poor often excel in the virtues of humility, submission, kindness, patience, and (interestingly) generosity. However, the rich also are quite prone to an inordinate delight in the things of this world, to arrogant independence from God, and to self-indulgent stinginess. The poor, on the other hand, constantly battle temptation in the form of inordinate desires for the things of this world, accusatory thoughts about God, and consuming self-pity.

In verse 4 of Chapter 5, James confronts the unrighteous rich with a sin representative of their godless attitude. "Behold, the pay of the laborers who mowed your fields, and which has been withheld by you, cries out against you; and the outcry of those who did the harvesting has reached the ears of the Lord of Sabaoth." The rich had been carried away and enticed by their lust for the things of the world; that lust had conceived an attitude of self-indulgent greed, which in turn had given birth to the act of defying God's laws. That attitude and behavior, if not confessed and forgiven, would lead to death. (See James 1:14–15.)

God had decreed in His Word that employers must deal with their employees *compassionately.* They were not to "oppress a hired servant . . . [but to] give him his wages on his day before the sun sets, for he is poor and sets his heart on it; so that he may not cry against you to the Lord and it become sin in you" (Deuteronomy 24:14–15). The prophet Jeremiah had warned against allowing self-indulgent greed to strangle compassion:

> *Woe to him who builds his house without righteousness*
> *And his upper rooms without justice,*
> *Who uses his neighbor's services without pay*
> *And does not give him his wages (22:13).*

And Malachi had made clear how God would respond when abused laborers cried out to Him in their distress: "'Then I will draw near to you for judgment; and I will be a swift witness against . . . those who oppress the wage earner in his wages . . . and do not fear Me,' says the Lord of hosts" (3:5).

Power, position, and wealth are always "on loan" from God. Wise stewards see them as a means of dispensing our Father's compassion to his needy children; however, fools like the ones James is addressing give in to their selfish passions and set themselves up for the judgment of God.

### Greed Never Wins

Self-indulgent greed is tragically foolish because it never wins. Perhaps in this case, the rather irreverent statement "God will get you for that" is entirely appropriate! The great Bible commentator Matthew Henry has explained: "The Lord of hosts, who has all ranks of beings and creatures at his disposal, and who sets all in their several places, hears the oppressed when they cry by reason of cruelty or injustice of the oppressor, and he will give orders to some of those hosts that are under him . . . to avenge the wrongs done to those who are dealt with unrighteously and unmercifully."[5]

*Lord of Sabaoth* is the name of God used in the Bible to describe His majestic power as ruler of the world and commander of the hosts of heaven.[6] James uses it here with good reason: He wants to underscore God's sovereign authority to judge the unrighteous, as well as His merciful goodness in defending the downtrodden. God, the all-powerful ruler, will surely condemn the greedy rich who have uselessly hoarded and self-indulgently spent their unjustly gained and ruthlessly acquired wealth.

God is the dispenser of all material goods. He bestows them for the purpose of exalting His glory. Those who foolishly disdain their stewardship privileges will pay a high price. And this truth applies to believers and unbelievers alike. Keep in mind that even though James is speaking about unbelievers in this part of his letter, he is also speaking to Christians. Therefore, his words have a definite double edge to them. They are both an encouraging reminder to the oppressed of God's certain judgment and a convicting warning to wealthy Christians against committing this sin.

James is not the only writer of Scripture who dwells on these issues. The Psalms are replete with encouragement for the abused, with Psalms 37 and 73 being two good examples. And the New Testament echoes with exhortations regarding the proper way to use wealth. Matthew and Luke record Jesus' teaching that no one can serve more than one master (Matthew 6:24; Luke 16:9–13). In Acts we see the early Church's sterling example of sharing to meet needs (4:32–35). Paul exhorted his protégé, Timothy, to "[i]nstruct those who are rich in this present world not to be conceited or to fix their hope on the uncertainty of riches, but on God, who richly supplies us with all things to enjoy. Instruct them to do good, to be rich in good works, to be generous and ready to share, storing up for themselves the treasure of a good foundation for the future, so that they may take hold of that which is life indeed" (1 Timothy 6:17–19). And John cautioned those who had "the world's goods" not to close their hearts against a "brother in need" (1 John 3:17–18).

There should be no doubt in our minds that those who, in James's words, have "lived luxuriously on the earth and led a life of wanton pleasure; . . . have fattened [their] hearts in a day of slaughter. . . . [and] condemned and put to death the righteous man" (5:5–6) are flagrantly violating God's commandments in Scripture. The righteous, however, should not lose heart and become discouraged. The Lord of Sabaoth is their powerful Sovereign, who always deals justly. In our next chapter, we'll see how they can live wisely in a "real world" full of distress by patiently trusting in Him.

[1] These verses were covered in depth in chapter 4 of *James on Trials.*

[2] James Montgomery Boice, *Developing a Christian Mind: Preparing People to Think and Act Biblically* (Philadelphia: The Bible Study Hour, nd), tape 2 of 4.

[3] John Blanchard, *Truth For Life: A Devotional Commentary on the Epistle of James* (Durham, England: Evangelical Press, 1986), 338.

[4] *Ibid.*

[5] Matthew Henry, *Matthew Henry's Commentary on the Whole Bible: Volume 6, Acts to Revelation* (Peabody, Mass.: Hendrickson Publishers, 1991), 801.

[6] D. Edmond Hiebert, *James* (Chicago: Moody Press, 1979, 1992), 266.

## Review Questions

1. How does Agur's prayer in Proverbs 30:8–9 relate to James's exhortation in 1:9–11 of his letter to those living in extreme financial conditions? Read James 5:1–12 in the light of Proverbs 30:8–9 and James 1:9–11; then explain how the rich and the poor each have special needs for God's wisdom.

2. Using the example of Nebuchadnezzar in Daniel 4:28–37, explain in your own words why trying to think outside of the context of God's absolute sovereignty amounts to insanity.

3. Describe "the madness of materialism." What is its only cure, according to John Blanchard? How does Nebuchadnezzar's example support John Blanchard's assertion?

4. List some of the peculiar blessings and curses of both wealth and poverty. Do you think walking worthy of their high calling in Christ is more difficult for the rich or for the poor? Explain your answer.

5. Summarize the requirements that God places on employers. Use the verses you studied in this chapter and any others of which you may be aware. Then relate the behavior of the employers whom James addresses in 5:4 to his earlier teaching in 1:14–15. What attitudes are revealed in their behavior?

---

6. What attributes of God are captured in the name *Lord of Sabaoth*? Why did James choose to use this name of God in his words to the ungodly rich?

7. Describe the encouragement and the warning to believers contained in James 5:1–6.

## Applying the Word

1. Read Psalms 37 and 73 carefully, filling in the following chart:

| God's specific instructions to believers | Ways in which God cares for His children | Ways in which God will deal with the wicked |
| --- | --- | --- |
| | | |

Are you being subjected to mistreatment, injustice, or oppression in your life right now? If so, briefly describe your situation. If not, do you know someone who is? If so, describe his or her situation.

How has your study of Psalms 37 and 73 deepened your understanding of God as the Lord of Sabaoth?

How will this deepened understanding of God help you think about your situation (or the situation of the person you know) within the context of God's absolute sovereignty?

How will this kind of thinking change your attitude toward your situation? Explain. How does it better equip you to help others who are in distress? Explain.

## Digging Deeper

1. According to Martin Luther, "It is God's nature to make something out of nothing, that is why He cannot make anything out of him who is not yet nothing." Relate his statement to what you have learned in Chapters Three and Four about the wisdom of submitting to God and the foolishness of arrogant independence.

*"A man with God on his side
is always in the majority."*

∞

John Knox

# Chapter Five

## *Genuine Wisdom Hopes Patiently*

---

*Be patient, therefore, brethren, until the coming of the Lord. Behold, the farmer waits for the precious produce of the soil, being patient about it, until it gets the early and late rains. You too be patient; strengthen your hearts, for the coming of the Lord is at hand. Do not complain, brethren, against one another, that you yourselves may not be judged; behold, the Judge is standing right at the door. As an example, brethren, of suffering and patience, take the prophets who spoke in the name of the Lord. Behold, we count those blessed who endured. You have heard of the endurance of Job and have seen the outcome of the Lord's dealings, that the Lord is full of compassion and is merciful. But above all, my brethren, do not swear, either by heaven or by earth or with any other oath; but let your yes be yes, and your no, no; so that you may not fall under judgment. (James 5:7–12)*

I'm sure you've heard evangelistic appeals that sound something like this: "What have you got to lose by becoming a Christian? If you receive Christ and there is an afterlife, you will spend it in heaven—but even if there isn't, your life here on earth will be much better with Him than without Him." Sounds like a logical, persuasive approach, right?

I always thought so until someone suggested I reread 1 Corinthians 15 to get Paul's perspective. And since Paul's perspective is certainly more important than mine, let me suggest that you do the same before you read on.

Did you discover, as I did, that "the world's greatest evangelist" didn't use the approach that sounds so persuasive and logical? First Corinthians 15:12–19, in particular. makes that fact very clear:

> *Now if Christ is preached, that He has been raised from the dead, how do some among you say that there is no resurrection of the dead? But if there is no resurrection of the dead, not even Christ has been raised; and if Christ has not been raised, **then our preaching is vain, your faith also is vain.** Moreover we are even found to be **false witnesses of God**, because we witnessed against God that He raised Christ, whom He did not raise, if in fact the dead are not raised. For if the dead are not raised, not even Christ has been raised; and if Christ has not been raised, **your faith is worthless; you are still in your sins.** Then those also who have fallen asleep in Christ have perished. If we have hoped in Christ **in this life only**, we are of all men most to be pitied"* (**bold** type added for emphasis).

Paul knew that preaching "What have you got to lose?" is vain and produces a *vain faith* for at least three reasons. First of all, such an approach misrepresents absolute truth by allowing the possibility that it might not be true. Paul persistently and consistently affirmed the undeniable fact of Christ's resurrection because to do anything else would make him *a false witness* of God (v. 15).

Secondly, this kind of preaching appeals to the short-sighted concerns of fallen humanity instead of to our real need—which is eternal. Even if having faith in an unresurrected Redeemer could help us live in happiness and contentment (and I'm not sure it could), it does not change the reality of an afterlife in which we will be judged. Christ's resurrection marks God's acceptance of full payment for the sins of His children. If it did not occur, then our faith is worthless because we are still in our sins (v. 17). And if we are still in our sins, we will be judged unfit to live in eternity with the God whose eyes are too pure to look upon evil and condone wrongdoing (Habakkuk 1:13).

Finally, Paul indicates that such preaching distorts the message of the Gospel by fixing our hope in this world instead of the next. Paul knew that this world is full of suffering, and that Christ had promised His followers more of the same (Matthew 5:10–12). Therefore, if we hope in Christ *in this life only*, we are of all people most to be pitied (1 Corinthians 15:19).

Of course, the great bedrock Gospel truth of Christ's resurrection supports our approach to wise Christian living just as well as it does our approach to evangelism. Our teacher, James, echoes Paul's thinking as he reminds suffering believers that their hope in Christ is anchored *not in this life only,* but in eternity. That is what gives them the patience to "suffer long" with those who abuse them.

### Wise Hope Builds Patient Faith

Genuine wisdom is rooted, grounded, and shot through with hope because it *enjoys* submitting to God's comforting sovereignty. Truly wise people are happy because they are humble. They know they were created dependent on God for every aspect of life, and their greatest satisfaction results from obedient trust. The scriptural truths they are learning about God and His work anchor their hope in His promises of future perfection rather than in this world's shaky foundations. The more secure their hope grows, the more patient their faith; and the more patient their faith, the greater their joy.

John Blanchard, in his book *Truth for Life,* alludes to this anchor of hope when he says, "Biblical patience is not rooted in fatalism that says everything is out of control. It is rooted in faith that says everything is in God's control."[1] As God's Holy Spirit deepens our understanding of His oversight of the distress in the world to accomplish His purposes, we learn to *hope joyfully* by looking beyond the things that are seen to the things that aren't seen (Isaiah 40:7–8; Jeremiah 29:11–13; 2 Corinthians 4:16–18).

Such God-centered hope equips us to obey our Father's command to "Rest in the Lord and wait patiently for Him" (Psalm 37:7)—in other words, to exercise wise, patient faith. Wise Christians know that God loves them too much to allow them to suffer without a good reason (Jeremiah 29:11; 31:3; Romans 8:32). They know that He will never leave them to suffer alone and unaided (Matthew 28:20; 1 Corinthians 10:13; Hebrews 13:5–6). And they know that all righteous suffering is temporary and generates a reward that is well worth the effort (Romans 8:18; 1 Peter 5:10).

Wise Christians have counted the cost of their discipleship and expect to suffer as a result of their obedience to the call of Christ. They welcome the assurance that builds as persecution and hardship test their allegiance to His perfection and power while it underscores His magnificent worth as full compensation and prize (Philippians 3:12–14). They understand Satan's desire to twist into something evil the suffering that God intended for good (Genesis 50:20); and they resist his attempts to pervert God's necessary good work of purifying our faith. Wise Christians agree with Paul's teaching that Christianity was never meant to be a good way to "maximize pleasure" in this present life (1 Corinthians 15:32). And they pronounce a hearty "Amen!" to James's assertion of our need for patience because we will not know maximum pleasure until the Lord Jesus returns.[2]

"Be patient, therefore, brethren," James now advises his readers, "until the coming of the Lord. Behold, the farmer waits for the precious produce of the soil, being patient about it, until it gets the early and late rains. You too be patient; strengthen your hearts, for the coming of the Lord is at hand" (5:7–8). The Greek word James uses here to refer to the Lord's second coming is *parousia*—a word that speaks of authority and power and is frequently used to describe the arrival of an emperor or king.[3] Knowledgeable Christians know that Christ first came in humility for the purpose of living and dying in subordination to God to secure our salvation. They know that His resurrection and ascension marked His exaltation to the right hand of God (Acts 2:33), where today He exercises "[a]ll authority . . . in heaven and on earth" (Matthew 28:18). And they know that He will come again in power to end the curse (Romans 8:20–21), overthrow evil (Revelation 20:10–15), and usher in God's eternal Kingdom (21:1–8).

Wise Christians, however, move beyond knowledge to application. They use what they know as the basis for hope that equips them to be patient in trying circumstances. Their patience does not take the form of fatalistic complacency, stoical insensitivity, nor irrational denials of evil's reality. Rather, it rejoices to submit every aspect of life to the God who is sovereign. Wise Christians display patient faith because they act upon God's revealed truth. They cast all their anxiety upon Him because they know He cares for them (1 Peter 5:7) and that He will perfect the good work He has begun in them (Philippians 1:6).

Just like a wise farmer who patiently accepts hardship and distress for the sake of a good crop, wise Christians "consider it all joy" when they patiently "suffer long" for the sake of God's promises. May we exercise that kind of wisdom!

### How Patience Behaves

The certainty of our faith in Christ's second coming not only equips us to wait patiently for it; it also shapes our behavior while we are waiting. George Bernard Shaw captured this characteristic of faith when he said, "Our conduct is influenced not so much by our experience as by our expectations."[4]

Wise patient faith is slow to anger (James 1:19–20) and doesn't complain (5:9) because it rests in the hopeful assurance of full vindication at Christ's Second Coming. Christians who exercise such faith do so with the understanding that God is the righteous Judge of the wicked as well as their loving Father. They can endure all things now because they have learned from the sterling examples of patient saints of the past that "the outcome of the Lord's dealings" reveals His compassion and mercy toward His chosen children (vv. 10–11).

Their attitude and behavior should not be construed as a validation of evil, nor as passive resistance to fate, but as purposeful self–restraint that draws on the power of God's Holy Spirit to resist hasty retaliation when they face provocation. Those who exercise wise, patient faith would agree with D. Edmond Hiebert when he asserts, "Christianity is strongly opposed to all forms of social injustice, but it also urges believers to maintain a proper attitude and perspective amid such injustices."[5] Wise, patient Christians submit to God's sovereign working of *all things*—even injustice and evil—together for good to accomplish His purposes (Genesis 50:20; Acts 2:23–24; Romans 8:28).

Having highlighted this truth in vv. 7–8, James cautions his readers against complaining (v. 9) and swearing (v. 12). He knew that impatience in tribulation leads to anger expressed in irritation, slander, and wrath against those who practice oppression. Such actions generate an atmosphere of discontentment and self-assertion, which fosters complaint against Christian brothers and sisters as well as self-reliant oath-taking. This kind of behavior interferes with the pursuit of the believers' chief end by robbing them of their joy and thus dishonoring God.

When we as Christians allow persecution and trouble to affect us this way, James says we can expect to be judged (v. 9). Of course, this "judgment" differs from what the wicked will bear, in that it is disciplinary and does not condemn us (Jeremiah 2:18–19; Romans 8:1; Hebrews 12:5–8; 1 Peter 4:17). James seems to be cautioning us to remember that even though discipline has value for our sanctification, it should be avoided if possible. Not only is it decidedly unpleasant, but it also sidelines us for a time from useful service to God.

When we exercise wise, patient faith by enduring all things in the hope of Christ's coming, we can rejoice with Asaph the psalmist, who proclaimed in the midst of difficulty and trial:

> *Whom have I in heaven but Thee?*
> *And besides Thee, I desire nothing on earth.*
> *My flesh and my heart may fail,*
> *But God is the strength of my heart and my portion*
>      *forever.*
> *For, behold, those who are far from Thee will perish;*
> *Thou hast destroyed all those who are unfaithful to Thee.*
> *But as for me, the nearness of God is my good;*
> *I have made the Lord God my refuge,*
> *That I may tell of all Thy works.  (Psalm 73:25–28)*

[1]   John Blanchard, T*ruth For Life: A Devotional Commentary on the Epistle of James* (Durham, England: Evangelical Press, 1986), 348.

[2]   Much of the information in this paragraph comes from Chapter 10 of John Piper's *Desiring God: Meditations of a Christian Hedonist* (Sisters Ore.: Multnomah Books, 1986, 1996). This chapter was added to the 1996 edition of Piper's thought-stirring book and contains many refreshing insights into the nature and purpose of suffering. If you haven't read it, I urge you to do so.

[3]   Blanchard, *Truth for Life*, 341.

[4]   Quoted in *ibid*, 343.

[5]   D. Edmond Hiebert, *James* (Chicago: Moody Press, 1979, 1992), 259. Original title, *The Epistle of James.*

# Review Questions

1. Reread 1 Corinthians 15 carefully and then use what you've read to respond to this question: "Would Paul have used (or approved of) the 'What have you got to lose?' method of evangelism?"

2. Describe the relationship between our hope in Christ and patient faith.

3. Explain how genuine wisdom generates joy. Support your reasoning with Scripture.

4. Write a brief character sketch of a Christian who has learned to exercise wise, patient faith.

5. James reminds his readers of the Lord's second coming as an incentive for them to exercise patience. Explain how this reminder motivates believers to be patient in difficulty.

6. Explain how George Bernard Shaw's words, "Our conduct is influenced not so much by our experience as by our expectations," summarize what James teaches in 5:9–12.

7. If you have not done so already, memorize Psalm 73:25–28

## Applying the Word

1. List five or more things (possibly including people) in which worldly minded people seek security. Then ask the Lord's help in prayer to examine your heart and discover how much you depend on these things for your security in this life. Describe the one(s) upon which you are most tempted to depend.

Read and meditate on Isaiah 40:3–31, Jeremiah 29:11–13; 2 Corinthians 4:7–18, and Philippians 3:1–14. In the spaces below summarize the teaching of each of these passages regarding the only legitimate source of your secure hope as a believer.

Isaiah 40:3–31:

Jeremiah 29:11–13:

2 Corinthians 4:7–18:

Philippians 3:1–14:

Now describe specific thoughts, attitudes, and behavior that you should change in order to begin seeking your security in the right places. Devise a step-by-step plan that will help you make one or more of these changes; then share your plan with someone who loves you enough to hold you accountable.

2. Describe three or more specific examples *from your own life* of how a secure hope in Christ's second coming will help you develop wise, patient faith. How will developing wise, patient faith equip you to minister to others in your family or your circle of friends? In answering this question, think about to whom you will minister, *when* and *where* you will minister to them, what you will do for them, and how (with what kind of attitude) you will minister to them.

3. For a period of one week, pay particular attention to your own speech with the intent of evaluating how much you complain. Listen carefully to the ways you respond verbally to people and events in your daily routine. Do your words reflect confident trust in God's sovereign control of every circumstance of life? Is your example as encouraging to other believers as that of the prophets and Job? What specific changes should you make in your speech in order to reflect more accurately the great power of God and to be a better example to others? How will you implement those needed changes?

## Digging Deeper

1. Two Greek words are frequently translated into English as patience. One is *makrothumeō*; the other is *hupomonē*. Using an exhaustive concordance, Bible dictionary, Greek lexicon, and/or other appropriate reference books, look up these two words and determine the differences in meaning between them. Then use an interlinear Bible (or the Greek text, if you know the language) and determine which of these two words James used in 1:2–3 and 5:7–8 of his letter. Given the context of these passages, explain James's choice of words (*makrothumeō* vs. *hupomonē*) in each of these instances. Be sure to include in your explanation what his pastoral as well as linguistic reasons might have been for using the words that he did.

*"It is good having those for friends
whose prayers are available
in the sight of God."*

Matthew Henry

# Chapter Six

# *Genuine Wisdom Prays*

---

*Is anyone among you suffering? Let him pray. Is anyone cheerful? Let him sing praises. Is anyone among you sick? Let him call for the elders of the church, and let them pray over him, anointing him with oil in the name of the Lord; and the prayer offered in faith will restore the one who is sick, and the Lord will raise him up, and if he has committed sins, they will be forgiven him. Therefore, confess your sins to one another, and pray for one another, so that you may be healed. The effective prayer of a righteous man can accomplish much. Elijah was a man with a nature like ours, and he prayed earnestly that it might not rain; and it did not rain on the earth for three years and six months. And he prayed again, and the sky poured rain, and the earth produced its fruit.* (James 5:13–18)

"Prayer is the antidote for the disease of self–confidence."[1]

That sentence is vintage John Piper. It packs the essence of why genuine wisdom prays into one concise sentence—and, in the process, packs quite a wallop. Piper has a rare gift for conveying a vast wealth of meaning in a paucity of words, as this sentence well illustrates. Indeed, everything that I'll be saying in this chapter, he concisely expresses here in ten simple words! But even so, I must urge you to resist the temptation of skipping straight to the questions. You see, one of the greatest delights in reading John Piper is pausing to "unpack" one of his loaded sentences.

I encountered this one while preparing to work through his book *Desiring God: Meditations of a Christian Hedonist* with my friend Angela. At the time, I was also researching this book on James. Perhaps that is why I was struck by the way Piper's sentence so aptly summarizes James's teaching on the wisdom of prayer.

Now if you're thinking, *I've just read James 5:13–18 and Piper's sentence, but I don't see the connection,* don't feel too bad. It helps to have read the ten pages he wrote about prayer that lead up to that sentence! In those pages he reminds us of several significant and helpful biblical truths. First and foremost, he reasserts God's intense interest in displaying the fullness of His own glory by "spilling over" that fullness in mercy to us.[2] The end result of that intense interest Piper expresses like this: "When we humble ourselves like little children and put on no airs of self-sufficiency, but run happily into the joy of our Father's embrace, the glory of His grace is magnified and the longing of our soul is satisfied."[3]

Piper then takes us to the Upper Room Discourse (John 13–16), where he revisits the facts that prayer is a means of pursuing God's glory (14:13), that it is also a means of pursuing our joy (16:24), and that it enables us to pursue both of those things by asking God to do for us through Christ what we can't do for ourselves (15:7). Piper elaborates on these great truths: "Prayer is the open admission that without Christ we can do nothing. And prayer is the turning away from ourselves to God in confidence that he will provide the help we need. Prayer humbles us as needy, and exalts God as wealthy."[4]

Piper also emphasizes that those who know Jesus best will ask the most from Him (because they best understand their own need and God's full provision [John 4:9–10]) and that when we "call upon [Him] in the day of trouble" we will be delivered, but He must get the glory (Psalm 50:15).[5]

Having said all that, Piper takes us to James 4:3–5. This passage, he says, pictures a kind of prayer that God will condemn. The Church is here portrayed as an unfaithful wife who seeks from the world the pleasures she should seek from her Husband (God) and then has the audacity to ask her Husband for the resources she needs to pursue her unfaithfulness. Piper's summary of James 4:3–5 is downright shocking: "We use our Husband's generosity to hire prostitutes for private pleasures."[6] But perhaps we need to be shocked. We all find it easier to pray "with wrong motives, so that [we] may spend it on our pleasures" (v. 3) than we do to pray with our hearts intent upon exalting God and delighting in Him.

Therefore, wise prayer *makes the effort* to acknowledge our own helplessness and His perfect power, to call upon

Him for the help that we desperately need to be righteous, and earnestly to seek His counsel concerning the affairs of our daily lives. It is at this point that Piper says, "Prayer is the antidote for the disease of self-confidence."

Are you beginning to see the connection between the teaching contained in James 5:13–18 and Piper's rich sentence? Genuine wisdom prays because it recognizes its utter dependence upon the Creator for every aspect of life. Prayer is thus an act of submission, which, we already have seen, is the key to wise living.

### "Prayer" Is the Right Answer to Every Question

If you grew up going to Sunday School, you may identify with the young boy who insightfully assured one nervous visitor, "Don't worry. No matter what question the teacher asks, the right answer is 'Jesus.'" But if you've thought through the verses that begin this chapter, you may be tempted to add, "Unless the teacher is James—then the right answer is 'prayer.'"

James asks his distressed readers three pertinent questions; then he answers each one with the same essential response.

Q: Is anyone among you suffering?
A: Let him pray.
Q: Is anyone cheerful?
A: Let him sing praises.[7]
Q: Is anyone among you sick?
A: Let him call for the elders of the church, and let them pray over him, anointing him with oil in the name of the Lord.

The first question is obviously rhetorical. James knew they were suffering. His awareness of and concern for their suffering prompted his letter. He already has spilled a great deal of ink reminding them of their all-sufficient resources in Christ, resources that will comfort and sustain them through the difficulties of life. He has described the nature of genuine faith and extolled the virtues of "the wisdom from above" as the means of living out their high calling in Christ. Now with characteristic practicality, he exhorts them to pray—not only in troubled times, but in all situations of life. Yes, of course, pray when you're suffering, he tells them. But also pray when you're happy, and when you're weak.

With these three questions, James emphasizes what our basic attitude should be toward life's mutability. No matter what comes our way, our response should be prayer. The Puritan Thomas Manton captured the key thought of James's teaching in this exquisite sentence: "It is the perfection of Christianity to have a constant mind in changing states."[8] Then he went on to affirm that the best way of acquiring and maintaining that constant mind is through consistent communion with the One who directs and controls those changing states.

Alec Motyer has expressed the same concept a bit more effusively: "Our whole life . . . should be so angled towards God that whatever strikes upon us, whether sorrow or joy, should be deflected upwards at once into His presence."[9] And David, on the day that the Lord delivered him from his enemies, voiced it poetically in Psalm 18:

> *"I love Thee, O Lord, my strength."*
> *The Lord is my rock and my fortress and my*
> *deliverer,*

> *My God, my rock, in whom I take refuge;*
> *My shield and the horn of my salvation, my*
>       *stronghold. . . .*
> *As for God, His way is blameless. . . .*
> *For who is God, but the* LORD?
> *And who is a rock, except our God,*
> *The God who girds me with strength,*
> *And makes my way blameless? . . .*
> *Thou hast also given me the shield of Thy*
>       *salvation,*
> *And Thy right hand upholds me. . . .*
> *The* LORD *lives, and blessed be my rock;*
> *And exalted be the God of my salvation. . . .*
> *Therefore I will give thanks to Thee among the*
>       *nations, O* LORD,
> *And I will sing praises to Thy name*
> *(vv. 1–2, 30, 31–32, 35, 46, 49).*

Faith at work turns every situation of life over to God in prayer, seeking the pure wisdom that infuses every situation with meaning and purpose. When we pray at all times with the help of His Spirit (Ephesians 6:18), we see our difficulties, delights, and weaknesses from His perspective instead of our own. And we trade the deadly disease of self-confidence for the glowing health of trusting fully in God (Psalm 40:4; Jeremiah 17:5–8).

### Some Controversial Verses

If you've been involved in Bible study for very long, you are no doubt aware that James 5:14–15 has generated great controversy within the Body of Christ. Protestants have long disagreed with Roman Catholics, who base their sacrament of extreme unction upon this passage. Some

Christians claim these verses as a guaranteed formula for miraculous physical healing, whereas others assert that James is not speaking of physical healing at all but is wholly concerned with our spiritual health. Other Christians admit they don't know who's right and who's wrong, but they take the "elder and oil" route when they are sick simply because the Bible commands it.

Well, if you are looking to me for the definitive answer, you're going to be disappointed. Since I am neither a trained theologian nor a church officer, I am not qualified to speak definitively on this thorny passage of Scripture. However, as a weak but Spirit-led lay person (just like most of you), I can and will give you two helpful guidelines for understanding these verses.

First and foremost, consider the passage within both its immediate and broader contexts. James is discussing the wisdom of prayer; therefore, the words in these verses must be consistent with what he (and the rest of the Bible) teaches about both wisdom and prayer. If you take the time to investigate the whole counsel of God on these two topics, you will discover that "wise prayer" looks exactly the way that James describes it: It is offered to God *in the name of the Lord*, and it is offered *in faith*. (See John 14:13–14, 15:16, 16:23–24; James 1:6–8; 1 John 3:21–22, 5:13–15.) In other words, such prayer is offered in accord with His mind, on His authority, and within His will.[10]

You will also discover that wise prayer is *effective* because its primary concern is the glory of God and the accomplishment of His purposes. John Blanchard describes it as "circular in shape; it begins and ends in heaven, in the sovereign will of God."[11]And D. Edmond Hiebert suggests that James's unconditional language in this passage is explained by the fact that wise prayer reflects God's will in the matter instead of the will of a person.[12] Therefore, prayers for healing will be effective when they reflect God's mind on the matter rather than ours.

The second guideline is to make use of some good reference books (or reliable commentaries) to learn all you can about the word "sick", the function of elders in the Church, and about the use of oil in the Middle East during the first century. Since so much of the controversy surrounding this passage hovers around those three things, you need to know that "sick" is the Greek word *asthenei*, which means "without strength"; that elders have been particularly called and gifted to speak to God on behalf of their flock; and that oil was used medicinally at that time and place. Those facts won't give you all the answers you want, but they will help you think clearly about what James is saying.

It seems to me that his words about healing urge believers to pray wisely in any and all weakness—be it physical, mental, moral, or spiritual—with two thoughts in mind: (1) A weakness in any one of these areas will eventually affect all the others, and (2) our weaknesses are intended to show forth God's glory by demonstrating His power, either in healing the weakness or in enabling us to serve Him effectively in weakness. Wise prayer seeks out and requests His will for each situation.

## The Effective Prayers of the Righteous

When we pray wisely, James assures us that God will answer. "[A]nd the prayer offered in faith (and in the name of the Lord; see v. 14) will restore the one who is sick, and the Lord will raise him up, and if he has committed sins, they will be forgiven him" (5:15).

Although that statement may sound astounding when pulled out of context, it is no more amazing than these words of John: "And this is the confidence which we have before Him, that, if we ask anything according to His will, He hears us. And if we know that He hears us in whatever we ask, we know that we have the requests which we have asked from Him" (1 John 5:14–15). Answered prayer should not come as a surprise to us, for we are God's children. Indeed, such a surprise may indicate that we are not in the habit of praying wisely.

Since God answers wise prayers, James tells us to "confess your sins to one another, and pray for one another, so that you may be healed. The effective prayer of a righteous man can accomplish much" (v. 16). The repeated reference to sin in verses 15–16 has led many competent commentators to the conclusion that James is limiting his assurances to spiritual healing—and they may be right. However, his concluding sentence in verse 16 has given me a slightly different perspective. Could he be saying that righteous people pray wisely (and thus effectively) because righteousness requires confession of sin—and that confession of sin enhances our ability to seek out and submit to God's will for a particular circumstance—and that when we pray for God's

will in that circumstance, He will answer our prayers? For
what it's worth, I give you that suggestion. Please act like
a Berean (see Acts 17:11) and also consider the opinions of
others more learned than I am before you accept it.

James caps his remarks about prayer with a stunning
example of what the righteous can do when they wisely
submit to God's purposes and then pray accordingly. If you
have not read 1 Kings 17–18 recently, please take a moment
to do so before going on. James's references to Elijah's
rain prayers  spotlight this portion of the Old Testament;
therefore, I am assuming that he intends the whole passage
to illustrate and support his teaching on prayer.

Did you notice the wide variety of miracles God
performed in response to the prayers of His servant, Elijah,
at that time in history? God not only controlled the weather,
created food, and raised a child from the dead (physical
miracles), but He also changed a woman's mind (a mental
miracle) and soundly defeated the prophets of Baal in a test
of strength (a spiritual miracle). Did you also notice that all
of these miraculous answers to prayer came because Elijah
prayed wisely in faith, being assured of God's will for the
situation? Surely that is why James refers us to him as a
prayer warrior worthy of our emulation.

[1]  John Piper, *Desiring God: Mediations of a Christian Hedonist*, ( Sisters,
Ore.: Multnomah Books, 1986, 1996), 146.

[2]  See Psalm 37 for an excellent biblical example of how the fullness of
God's glory spills over in mercy to His children.

[3]  Piper, *Desiring God*, 137.

4   Ibid, 138.

5   Ibid, 139–140.

6   Ibid, 141.

7   Although James doesn't use the word *pray* in this response, we can
    infer it safely. The Bible consistently teaches that praise and worship
    of God is the central element of righteous prayer. For a fuller discus-
    sion of this subject, see Lesson 5 of my book *Before the Throne of God:
    Focus on Prayer,* Light for Your Path Series (Phillipsburg, NJ: P & R
    Publishing, 1999).

8   Thomas Manton, *The Crossway Classic Commentaries: James,* series
    editors Alister McGrath and J. I. Packer (Wheaton, Ill.: Crossway
    Books, 1995), 328.

9   Quoted in John Blanchard, *Truth For Life: A Devotional Commentary
    on the Epistle of James* (Durham, England: Evangelical Press, 1986),
    363.

10  See my Light for Your Path study *Before the Throne of God: Focus on
    Prayer* (referenced at 7 above) for a fuller discussion of these issues.

11  Blanchard, *Truth for Life,* 377.

12  D. Edmond Hiebert, *James* (Chicago: Moody Press, 1979, 1992), 297.
    Original title, *The Epistle of James.*

## Review Questions

1. John Piper said, "Prayer is the antidote for the disease of self-confidence." In your own words, briefly explain how his words capture concisely the wisdom of prayer. Feel free to draw on what you have learned in previous chapters as well as in this one.

2. List the three occasions to which James says we should respond with prayer. (If you haven't read footnote [7], do so now.) Why do you think James chose these three situations to emphasize the wisdom of prayer?

3.  What do the quotations from Thomas Manton, Alec Motyer, and David on page 353  tell us about the wisdom of prayer?

4.  Explain how the two guidelines listed below help us understand James's teaching in the controversial verses, 5:14–15:

    The guideline of context:

    The guideline of key words and concepts:

5. What does wise prayer "look like" and what makes it effective? Read John 14:13–14, 15:16, 16:23–24; James 1:6–8; 1 John 3:21–22, 5:13–15 before attempting to answer this question and support your answer using those verses.

6. Describe the relationship between forgiveness of sin and wise prayer. Can an unrighteous person pray wisely? Why or why not?

7. Drawing on what you read in 1 Kings 17–18, explain why Elijah is a prayer warrior worthy of our emulation.

## Applying the Word

1. Using the following chart, list what you consider to be your primary strengths and weaknesses physically, mentally, morally, and spiritually. (HINT: A weakness is not a sin; see 2 Corinthians 12:7–10.) Before you begin, ask God to help you examine yourself (Psalm 139:23–24; Jeremiah 17:9–10). Be specific and current in your evaluation.

|  | Strengths | Weaknesses |
|---|---|---|
| Physical |  |  |
| Mental |  |  |
| Moral |  |  |
| Spiritual |  |  |

Consider your completed chart carefully; then answer the following questions.

Do you see evidence of a strength or weakness in one area affecting other areas? If so, explain.

How might each strength and weakness tempt you to sin?

How might each strength and weakness glorify God?

What was God's purpose in creating you with this particular set of strengths and weaknesses? (See Psalm 139 and recall the Westminster Shorter Catechism, Q/A 1.)

Select at least one weakness that is particularly distressing for you right now and write a wise prayer concerning it based upon what you have learned in these six chapters of study. Pray this prayer consistently during this week and record any resulting changes that you detect in your attitude and/or behavior.

# Digging Deeper

1. Describe the controversy surrounding James 5:14–15. Before you studied this chapter, did you have an opinion as to what James is teaching in these verses? If so, what was it? If your opinion has changed after studying this chapter, explain both the change and how the change came about. Support your opinion with Scripture.

*"I believe there is scarcely
an error in doctrine
or a failure in applying Christian ethics
that cannot be traced finally
to imperfect and ignoble
thoughts about God."*

∞

A. W. Tozer

# Chapter Seven

# *Genuine Wisdom Exhorts*

---

*My brethren, if any among you strays from the truth, and one turns him back, let him know that he who turns a sinner from the error of his way will save his soul from death, and will cover a multitude of sins. (James 5:19–20)*

James's little epistle to suffering believers "dispersed abroad" (1:1) ends rather abruptly. There is no verbal signal—no *therefore* or *finally*—to alert us to the fact that he has completed his message. There are none of the usual "greetings" that close the majority of New Testament letters. And there is no obvious link between Elijah's exemplary prayers and James's last words. We definitely get the impression that something is missing. Has part of this letter been lost? Was James interrupted before he finished his thoughts? We simply don't know.

Of this, however, we can be certain: Every word of this letter that God wants us to read has been preserved (Deuteronomy 29:29). And it has been recorded precisely as He intended. Since God in His sovereignty has controlled the writing of Scripture (Romans 15:4; 2 Timothy 3:14–17; 2 Peter 1:20–21), we know that nothing "pertaining to life and godliness" (2 Peter 1:3) has slipped through the cracks. Therefore, wisdom suggests that we pay heed to what is here instead of engaging in vain speculations about what might be missing (Titus 3:9).

I think you will find, as I have, that pausing to ponder James's final sentence in humble submission to God's revelation yields a rich harvest of insight. Although at first glance we may detect only one last piece of advice for the good of the Church, upon closer inspection we unearth a bit more. These words also lay bare the humble *heart* of genuine wisdom while defending the boldness with which James had written.

Genuine wisdom is energized by its great love for others. It selflessly seeks after the highest good of a neighbor. Therefore, it does not hesitate to exhort the wayward. Genuine wisdom knows that straying from truth produces no good and that bold action is needed to turn wayward sinners from their errors. James was a man who possessed genuine wisdom and was thereby motivated to write the bold letter that we have studied. So far he has called us to adhere to God's truth in every situation of life; now he exhorts us to join him in the wise task of exhorting others.

### The Value of Exhortation

James was an exhorter; that is, he concentrated upon calling people to live wisely by turning from their sinful ways to serve God in righteousness. James exhorted well because, like so many other writers of Scripture, he was a master of balancing conviction with comfort.

Exhortation in Scripture has to do with encouraging or, in other words, infusing courage or building strength to accomplish God's purposes.[1] It is a fascinating, multi-faceted concept that encompasses teaching, admonition, correction, and discipline as well as compassion, consolation, understanding, and motivation. Please note my emphasis on the word encompass, which means "to contain, surround, or encircle." Exhortation does not pick and choose among the activities listed; it wraps its powerful, loving arms around all of them!

Perhaps that is why so few Christians these days accept James's charge to exhort others biblically—and why the Church as a whole is lacking courage and strength. Exhortation is difficult; it requires patient endurance, knowledge of Scripture, and bold dependence on God. Most of us would simply rather not make such a great effort. Unfortunately, opting for ease doesn't benefit anyone. If we were all more adept at dispensing (and receiving!) fully orbed biblical exhortation, the Body of Christ would be built up mightily. But let's not sit around lamenting the problem when our time would be better spent examining James's example with the intent of accepting his challenge. How can his letter help us become better exhorters?

Do you remember the startling sentence with which James opened his letter? *Consider it all joy, my brethren, when you encounter various trials, knowing that the testing of your faith produces endurance* (1:2–3). That is a masterpiece of fully orbed biblical exhortation! And we can learn a great deal by analyzing it carefully. Before you read on, take a few minutes to note which "facets" of exhortation listed above you can spot in that sentence.

I'm sure that all of you grammar mavens recognized the imperative mood of the verb *consider*, which classifies the whole sentence as a command. Even if you aren't a grammar maven, you know that commands are associated with *admonitions and/or corrections.* They are issued in recognition of a need for change. It would be rather silly and pointless to command people to do what they are already doing!

Since commands call for a change of some sort, they demand obedience. And obedience depends upon teaching and discipline. Before James's readers will be able to effectively obey his command, they must be *taught* what, where, when, and how they are to obey; and they must exercise *discipline* (and perhaps even be disciplined) to put what they learn into practice.

But James is no heartless first sergeant, barking orders to people he doesn't care much about. He is writing to members of his spiritual family—and he loves them all dearly. Therefore, he not only commands them to do what is in their best interests but also consoles them with hope instead of frail sympathy. You may have noticed that James doesn't pat his readers figuratively on the back while murmuring, "Oh, you poor little things." Rather, he boldly presents them with his *understanding* of how their situation fits perfectly within God's purposes for them. They can and should consider trials as "all joy" because God uses them to build up the faith of His children.

Encouraging his distressed readers with this hopeful truth is an expression of James's wise compassion for them. It is important to know that compassion acts on another's behalf and thus moves beyond both sympathy (feelings of sorrow for another) and empathy (mental identification with someone else's situation). Sympathizing with people is good, and empathizing with them is better, but extending compassion toward them is best—and it is essential to exhortation because it fuels motivation. Whereas sympathy and empathy give hurting people a welcome shoulder to cry on, compassion helps them overcome their distress by pointing out the solution.

Of course, these three tools motivate best when they work together. When sympathy and empathy are unwisely extended, devoid of compassion, hurting people are often "encouraged" to sink into self-pity; and cold-hearted compassion comes across as so unloving and harsh that it typically motivates the distressed toward angry defensiveness. James, the master exhorter, skillfully wove all three together in the first words of his letter. His heartfelt identification with the plight of his readers is seen in the warm emotional phrase *my brethren*. And his wise compassion for them exudes from his bold, active directive to look at their circumstances from God's perspective.

Are you beginning to appreciate James's skill as an exhorter? If we had more time and energy, I'm sure we could analyze each sentence we've studied in his little letter just as we have his first one, but you can relax because we won't! What we will do instead is take a broad look at his overall exhortation to believers in Christ as a means of reviewing what we have learned in this *Faith at Work* series.

*James's Epistle—One Long Exhortation*

Yesterday I ran into a friend I hadn't seen in a couple of months, and one of the first things he asked me was, "How are you doing on James?" I told him that I was working on the last chapter  and that I was truly excited to have seen the <u>final sentence as both a summary and a defense of everything in the letter.</u> My friend was intrigued and asked me to explain. What a great opportunity that was to sort out my thoughts for writing this section!

I told my friend some of what I've already told you—that James 5:19–20 is where it is in this letter because God put it there, and that our job as wise readers of Scripture is to seek out His purpose for placing these words at the end of this letter. Since they describe the practice of exhortation and are included in a discussion of wise Christian living, we can deduce that exhortation is something wise Christians should practice. The fact that these words serve as the conclusion to James's letter could indicate that they summarize and defend his purpose and method of writing. And as I had thought back over the letter, I realized just how well they had done that.

<u>The epistle of James is one long exhortation that ends with an exhortation to exhort others in the same way in which you have been exhorted because exhortation lies at the heart of wise Christian living.</u> Whew! Did you get that? Let's go back and take a big-picture look at this letter so that we can better understand James's last words to his beloved, suffering brethren.

You remember, of course, that <u>James wrote to believers who had been forced to flee from Jerusalem in the wake</u>

of intense persecution. (See Acts 8:1–4.) As they settled among strangers in foreign lands, they faced a variety of difficulties that produced a great deal of distress and discouragement. James, as the leader of the church in Jerusalem, had remained in residence there, but his heart was with the scattered believers. Since he could not assist them face to face, he wrote them this letter. And he chose as his primary means of assistance the strong tool of exhortation.

We have already seen how James's opening sentence sets the balanced convicting/comforting tone of the letter by lovingly directing his readers to look at their situation from God's perspective. The very next sentence assures them of the wisdom of that kind of behavior: It will make them "perfect and complete, lacking in nothing" (1:4).

James then begins teaching his readers how to acquire the wisdom they need to overcome distressing circumstances. They must wholeheartedly seek it from God, who will give it to them "generously and without reproach" (1: 5–8). They must rely solely on spiritual resources while persevering through trials, because the crown of life waits for those who do (vv. 9–12). They must never accuse God of using trials to tempt them to sin; rather, they must realize that trials degenerate from tests (designed by God to strengthen) to temptations (designed by Satan to weaken) when those enduring the trial are "carried away and enticed by [their] own lust" (vv. 13–15). They must guard against the deception of the world, the flesh, and the devil by remembering that all things come into their lives by God's design and under His control for the good dual purpose of His exaltation and their edification (vv. 17–18).

Now that they have learned these truths, readers must put them into practice. James tells them that righteousness does not result from responding in anger to God's sovereign providence, but rather from "putting aside all filthiness and all that remains of wickedness," from humbly receiving "the word implanted," and from proving themselves "doers of the word, and not merely hearers" (vv. 19–25). True religion, implanted by God's revealed truth, will be reflected in the way they treat others—in both word and deed (1:26–2:13; 3:1–12). That is because genuine faith works in the power of God. Faith without righteous works is a contradiction in terms, and is characteristic of demons (2:14–26).

Those whose faith works to accomplish God's purposes are truly wise. They walk righteously and at peace with one another because they submit humbly to God and resist the devil (3:13–4:10). Their habitual responses to the stresses and strains of daily living reflect a God-centered focus that both honors Him and fills up their joy (4:11–5:18). Since they have both learned and applied what they have been taught, their next step is to exhort (that is, to encourage by teaching, admonishing, correcting, disciplining, extending compassion, consoling, understanding, and motivating) their brothers and sisters to come and do likewise (5:19–20).

### From Exhorted to Exhorter

Even though James's directive is clear, most Christians I know shy away (or even recoil!) from exhorting others. When I ask them why, they usually mumble something about "being tolerant of those who hold different opinions" or declare that they just aren't "qualified" to do such a thing.

Now at first blush, those answers may seem very loving and humble—but let's think for a moment about whether they really are so.

Do we love others by tolerating, ignoring, or even encouraging their descent into error? Do we act in humility by coming up with excuses for not doing what God clearly tells us to do in His Word? Scripture answers "No" to both questions. James himself tells us that taking action to turn "a sinner from the error of his way will save his soul from death, and will cover a multitude of sins" (5:19). Doesn't such behavior reflect the highest possible love for another? And since Paul says that every word of the Bible has been recorded for our instruction in righteousness and to give us hope (2 Timothy 3:16–17; Romans 15:4), shouldn't we follow James's exhortative example? We must answer "Yes" to both questions.

Paul echoes James's teaching that wise Christian living includes exhortation when he instructs the Galatians, "Brethren, even if a man is caught in any trespass, you who are spiritual, restore such a one in a spirit of gentleness; each one looking to yourself, lest you too be tempted" (Galatians 6:1). Those who are spiritual are those who read and apply God's truth in their lives. In the words of our Savior, they are those who have taken the log out their eye so that they can see clearly to take the speck out of the eye of a wayward brother or sister (Matthew 7:2–5).

The Church of Jesus Christ will be built up and strengthened when its individual members (that's you and I!) listen to God and do what He says. We can do that without fear because His commands are not burdensome. He is our loving Father, who loves us perfectly and knows what we need. Therefore, He exhorts us in His Word, through writers like James, to live wisely in humble dependence upon Him. Obeying such exhortation glorifies God and enhances our joy as we "work out our salvation" in pursuit of His purposes in our daily lives.

But our new life in Christ cannot be worked out effectively in isolation from the rest of the family. James has both exemplified for us and exhorted us to accept the essential task of encouraging others just as we have been encouraged. Will we make excuses—or do what he says? Will we prove ourselves doers of the word—or merely hearers? Will Christ's Church increase in courage and strength because we have heeded James's exhortation—or will it grow more fearful and weak because we have ignored him?

I say, let's join together in renewed commitment to walk worthy of our high calling in Christ by living wisely in the light of God's revealed truth!

---

[1] Lawrence O. Richards, *Expository Dictionary of Bible Words*, s. v. "encourage." Grand Rapids: Regency Reference Library, 1985.

## Review Questions

1. In your own words, describe *exhortation*. Then briefly explain exhortation's place in wise Christian living.

*encouraging others by teaching, correcting, admonishing, disciplining, extending compassion, consoling, understanding + motivating them to walk righteously + honor God c their lives + actions; motivated by love and provides hope + purpose in whatever the situation*

2. Explain how James's final sentence can be seen as (1) good advice for the Church, (2) the "purpose statement" of his letter, and (3) a defense of the boldness with which he wrote. (NOTE: A "purpose statement" reveals the author's reason[s] for writing. See Lesson 4 of my Light for Your Path study, *Turning on the Light*, for more information about purpose statements.)

*genuine wisdom is energized by great love for others → seeks their highest good → ∴ doesn't hesitate to exhort wayward (straying from truth requires bold action)*

*p.370 1) adhere to God's truth in every situation of life*
*2) join him in wise exhortation of others*

*371 because exhortation difficult, requires patient endurance, knowledge of scripture + total dependence*

3. How does good, biblical exhortation balance conviction with comfort? Why do you think it is important to balance conviction with comfort?

*p. 371*

4. Describe how James balances conviction with comfort in the opening sentence of his letter (1:2–3) as he addresses believers who have been dispersed abroad.

*p. 372 presents them c his understanding of how their situation fits perfectly c God's purposes for them → God uses trials to build up their faith*

5. Distinguish between sympathy, empathy, and compassion. Which of these tools is most effective in motivating believers to apply scriptural truth in their lives? Explain your answer.

p. 372 - 373

sympathy - feelings of sorrow for another

empathy - mental identification c̄ someone else's situation

compassion - help to overcome distress by pointing out a solution → consolation c̄ hope (p. 372)

looks at circumstances from God's perspective

6. Read through the book of James and record phrases and sentences that exhort believers in the following ways. (NOTE: If you are unsure of the meanings of the following words, look them up in a dictionary before you begin. Also be aware that many phrases and sentences in the book of James can be placed reasonably in more than one category.)

Teaching: *the act, practice, or profession of giving instruction PS 5I*

Admonition: *a gentle or friendly reproof; warning or counsel vs. fault or oversight  I Cor. 4:14*

Correction: *to set right (a person) II Tim 3:16*

Discipline: *to train; to bring into control; to chastise  I Cor. 9:24-27*

Compassion: *see question 5*

Consolation: *comfort in distress (solace); alleviation of misery  Ps. 94*

Understanding: *sympathetically discerning  I John 5:20*

Motivation: *incentive; motive is something (as a need or desire) that causes a person to act*

7. How does shying away or recoiling from exhortation reveal a lack of love and humility on the part of a believer?

p. 371
p. 373

5:1-6

1:13-20
1:18-b
2:4.6
3:1-4
4:15-17
4:15

## Applying the Word

1. Read through the book of James once again and then look over your answer to Review Question 6. Prayerfully consider which of the many exhortations contained in this epistle convict you regarding your walk with the Lord. List at least three of those below. Then list the exhortations that you find most comforting.

Regarding the areas in which you have been convicted, what does the book of James teach you to do? How does it admonish and correct you? How must you exercise self-discipline in these areas? What kind of discipline may you expect from God if you take no action in these areas?

Regarding the areas in which you have been comforted, how has James acted compassionately toward you? How has he consoled you? How has he indicated that he understands your situation? In what ways has he motivated you to act and think differently?

Describe at least three ways in which your life will change (or has changed already) as a result of having studied the book of James.

# Digging Deeper

1.  A. W. Tozer said, "I believe there is scarcely an error in
    doctrine or a failure in applying Christian ethics that cannot
    be traced finally to imperfect and ignoble thoughts about
    God." Would James have agreed with Tozer? Explain your
    answer thoroughly.

# *Recommended Reading*

Jay Adams, *A Thirst for Wholeness*. Wheaton, Ill.: Victor Books, 1988.

Jay Adams, *The Grand Demonstration: A Biblical Study of the So-Called Problem of Evil*. Santa Barbara, Calif.: East Gate Publishers, 1991

John Blanchard, *Truth for Life: A Devotional Commentary on the Epistle of James*. Durham, England: Evangelical Press, 1986.

Robert Bolton, *General Directions for a Comfortable Walking With God*. Originally published, 1626; reprint, Religious Tract Society, 1837; reprint, Ligonier, Penn.: Soli Deo Gloria Publications, 1991.

Jerry Bridges, *Transforming Grace: Living Confidently in God's Unfailing Love*. Colorado Springs: Navpress, 1991.

_____ *The Joy of Fearing God*. Colorado Springs: Water Brook Press, 1997.

_____ *The Pursuit of Holiness*. Colorado springs: Navpress, 1978.

_____ *The Practice of Godliness*. Colorado Springs: Navpress, 1983.

D. Edmond Hiebert, *James*. Chicago: Moody Press, 1979, 1992. (original title: *The Epistle of James*).

Michael Horton, *Made in America: The Shaping of Modern American Evangelicalism*. Grand Rapids: Baker Books, 1991.

John F. MacArthur, Jr., *Faith Works: The Gospel According to the Apostles.* Dallas: Word Publishing, 1993.

_____ *The Vanishing Conscience.* Dallas: Word Publishing Company, 1994.

J. Gresham Machen, *The Christian View of Man.* Carlisle, Penn.: The Banner of Truth Trust, 1984 (first published: 1937)

John Murray, *Principles of Conduct.* Grand Rapids: Wm. B. Eerdmans Publishing, 1957.

John Piper, *Desiring God: Meditations of a Christian Hedonist.* Sisters, Ore.: Multnomah Books, 1986, 1996

Carol J. Ruvolo, *Before the Throne of God: Focus on Prayer.* Phillipsburg, N.J.: P & R Publishing, 1999. (The Light for Your Path Series)

J. C. Ryle, *Practical Religion.* Carlisle, PA: The Banner of Truth Trust, 1998. (first published: 1878)

Edith Schaeffer, *Affliction.* Old Tappan, NJ: Fleming H. Revell Company, 1978.

Joni Eareckson Tada and Steven Estes, *When God Weeps: Why Our Sufferings Matter to the Almighty.* Grand Rapids: Zondervan Publishing House, 1997.

A. W. Tozer, *The Pursuit of God.* Camp Hill, PA: Christian Publications, Inc., 1982.

Edward T. Welch, *When People Are Big and God Is Small.* Phillipsburg, N.J.: P & R Publishing, 1997.

# Appendix A

# What Must I Do to Be Saved?

---

A strange sound drifted through the Philippian jail as midnight approached. It was the sound of human voices—but not the expected groans of the two men who earlier had been beaten with rods and fastened in stocks. Rather, the peaceful singing of praises to their God floated through the cells.

While the other prisoners quietly listened to them, the jailer dozed off, content with the bizarre calm generated by these two preachers, who had stirred so much commotion in the city just hours before.

Suddenly a deafening roar filled the prison, and the ground began to shake violently. Sturdy doors convulsed and popped open. Chains snapped and fell at prisoners' feet. Startled into full wakefulness, the jailer stared, horrified, at the wide-open doors that guaranteed his prisoners' escape—and his own death. Under Roman law, jailers paid with their lives when prisoners escaped. Resolutely, he drew his sword, thinking it better to die by his own hand than by Roman execution.

"Stop! Don't harm yourself—we are all here!" a voice

boomed from the darkened inner cell. The jailer called for lights and was astonished to discover his prisoners standing quietly amid their broken chains. Trembling with fear, he rushed in and fell at the feet of the two preachers. As soon as he was able, he led them out of the ruined prison and asked in utter astonishment, "Sirs, what must I do to be saved?"

In the entire history of the world, no one has ever asked a more important question. The jailer's words that day may well have been motivated by his critical physical need, but the response of Paul and Silas addressed his even more critical spiritual need: "Believe in the Lord Jesus, and you shall be saved, you and your household."[1]

If you have never "believed in the Lord Jesus," your spiritual need, just like the jailer's, is critical. As long as your life is stained with sin, God cannot receive you into His presence. The Bible says that sin has placed a separation between you and God (Isaiah 59:2). It goes on to say that your nature has been so permeated by sin that you no longer have any desire to serve and obey God (Romans 3:10–12); therefore, you are not likely to recognize or care that a separation exists. Your situation is truly desperate because those who are separated from God will spend eternity in hell.

Since your sinful nature is unresponsive to God, the only way you can be saved from your desperate situation is for God to take the initiative. And this He has done! Even though all men and women deserve the punishment of hell because of their sin, God's love has prompted Him to save some who will serve Him in obedience. He did this by sending His Son, the Lord Jesus Christ, to remove the barrier of sin between God and His chosen ones (Colossians 2:13–14).

What is there about Jesus that enables Him to do this? First of all, He is God. While He was on earth He said, "He who has seen Me has seen the Father" (John 14:9) and "I and the Father are one" (John 10:30). Because He said these things, you must conclude one of three things about His true identity: (1) He was a lunatic who believed he was God when he really wasn't; (2) He was a liar who was willing to die a hideous death for what he knew was a lie; or (3) His words are true and He is God.

Lunatics don't live the way Jesus did, and liars don't die the way He did; so if the Bible's account of Jesus' life and words is true, you can be sure He *is* God.

Since Jesus is God, He is perfectly righteous and holy. God's perfect righteousness and holiness demands that sin be punished (Ezekiel 18:4), and Jesus' perfect righteousness and holiness qualified Him to bear the punishment for the sins of those who will be saved (Romans 6:23). Jesus is the only person who never committed a sin; therefore, the punishment He bore when He died on the cross could be accepted by God as satisfaction of His justice in regard to the sins of others.

If someone you love commits a crime and is sentenced to die, you may offer to die in his place. However, if you also have committed crimes worthy of death, your death cannot satisfy the law's demands for your crimes *and* your loved one's. You can die in his place only if you are innocent of any wrongdoing.

Since Jesus lived a perfect life, God's justice could be satisfied by allowing Him to die for the sins of those who will be saved. Because God is perfectly righteous and holy, He could not act in love at the expense of justice. By sending Jesus to die, God demonstrated His love *by acting to satisfy His own justice* (Romans 3:26).

Jesus did more than die, however; He also rose from the dead. By raising Jesus from the dead, God declared that He had accepted Jesus' death in the place of those who will be saved. Because Jesus lives eternally with God, those for whom Jesus died can be assured that they also will spend eternity in heaven (John 14:1–3). The separation of sin has been removed!

Ah, but the all-important question remains unanswered: What must *you do* to be saved? If God has sent His Son into the world for sinners, and Jesus Christ died in their place, what is left for you to do? You must respond in faith to what God has done. This is what Paul meant when he told the jailer, "Believe in the Lord Jesus, and you shall be saved."

Believing in the Lord Jesus demands three responses from you: (1) an understanding of the facts regarding your hopeless sinful condition and God's action to remove the sin barrier that separates you from Him; (2) acceptance of those facts as true and applicable to you; and (3) a willingness to trust and depend upon God to save you from sin. This involves willingly placing yourself under His authority and acknowledging His sovereign right to rule over you.

But, you say, how can I do this if sin has eliminated my ability to know and appreciate God's work on my behalf? Rest assured that if you desire to have the sin barrier that separates you from God removed, He already is working to change your natural inability to respond. He is extending His gracious offer of salvation to you and will give you the faith to receive it.

If you believe that God is working to call you to Himself, read the words He has written to you in the Bible (perhaps beginning with the book of John in the New Testament) and pray that His Holy Spirit will help you understand what is written there. Continue to read and pray until you are ready to *repent*—that is, to turn away from sin and commit yourself to serving God.

Is there any other way you can be saved? God Himself says no, there is not. The Bible He wrote says that Jesus is the only way in which the sin barrier between you and God can be removed (John 14:6; Acts 4:12). He is your hope, and He is your *only* hope.

If you have questions or need any help in this matter, please write to The Evangelism Team, Providence Presbyterian Church, P. O. Box 14651, Albuquerque, NM 87191, before the day is over. God has said in His Bible that a day of judgment is coming, and after that day no one will be saved (Acts 17:30–31; 2 Thessalonians 1:7–9). The time to act is now.

---

[1] For a full biblical account of this event, see Acts 16:11–40.

# Appendix B

# What Is the Reformed Faith?

The term *the Reformed Faith*[1] can be defined as a theology that describes and explains the sovereign God's revelation of His actions in history to glorify Himself by redeeming selected men and women from the just consequences of their self-inflicted depravity.

It is first and foremost *theology* (the study of God), not *anthropology* (the study of man). Reformed thinking concentrates on developing a true knowledge of God that serves as the necessary context for all other knowledge. It affirms that the created world, including humanity itself, cannot be accurately understood apart from its relationship with the Creator.

The Reformed Faith describes and explains God's revelation of Himself and His actions to humanity; it does not consist of people's attempts to define God as they wish. The Reformed Faith asserts that God has revealed Himself in two distinct ways: He reveals His existence, wisdom, and power through the created universe—a process known as *natural revelation* (Romans 1:18–32); and He reveals His requirements and plans for mankind through His written Word, the Bible—a process known as *special revelation* (2 Timothy 3:16–17).

Reformed theologians uphold the Bible as the inspired, infallible, inerrant, authoritative, and fully sufficient communication of truth from God to humanity. When they call the Bible *inspired*, they mean that the Bible was actually written by God through the agency of human authorship in a miraculous way that preserved the thoughts of God from the taint of human sinfulness (2 Peter 1:20–21). When they call the Bible *infallible*, they mean that it is *incapable* of error. When they call it *inerrant*, they mean that the Bible, *in actual fact*, contains no errors. The Bible is authoritative because it comes from God, whose authority over His creation is absolute (Isaiah 46:9–10). And it is completely sufficient because it contains everything necessary for us to know and live according to God's requirements (2 Peter 1:3–4).

By studying God's revelation of Himself and His work, Reformed theologians have learned two foundational truths that structure their thinking about God's relationship with human beings: God is absolutely sovereign, and people are totally depraved.[2]

Reformed thought affirms that God, by definition, is absolutely sovereign—that is, He controls and superintends every circumstance of life, either by direct miraculous intervention or by the ordinary outworking of His providence. Reformed theologians understand that a "god" who is not sovereign cannot be God because his power would not be absolute. Since the Reformed Faith accepts the Bible's teaching regarding the sovereignty of God, it denies that *anything* occurs outside of God's control.

The Reformed Faith affirms the biblical teaching that Adam was created with the ability to sin and that he chose to sin by disobeying a clear command of God (Genesis 3:1–7). Choosing to sin changed basic human nature and left us unable not to sin—or *totally depraved.* Total depravity does not mean that all people are as bad as they possibly could be, but that every facet of their character is tainted with sin, leaving them incapable and undesirous of fellowship with God. The Reformed Faith denies that totally depraved men and women have any ability to seek after or submit to God of their own free will. Left to themselves, totally depraved men and women will remain out of fellowship with God for all eternity.

The only way for any of these men and women to have their fellowship with God restored is for God Himself to take the initiative. And the Bible declares that He has graciously chosen to do so (John 14:16). *For His own glory,* He has chosen some of those depraved men and women to live in fellowship with Him. His choice is determined by His own good pleasure and not by any virtue in the ones He has chosen. For this reason, *grace* is defined in Reformed thought as "unmerited favor."

God accomplished the salvation of His chosen ones by sending His Son, the Lord Jesus Christ, to bear God's righteous wrath against sin so that He could forgive those He had chosen. Even though Christ's work was perfect and complete, its effectiveness is limited to those who are chosen by God for salvation. Christ would not have been required to suffer any more or any less had a different number been chosen for redemption, but the benefit of His suffering is applied only to those who are called by God to believe in Him. And all those who are effectually called by God eventually will believe and be saved, even though they may resist for a time (John 6:37). They cannot forfeit the salvation they have received (John 10:27–30; Romans 8:31–39).

Reformed thought affirms the clear teaching of the Bible that salvation is by faith alone through Christ alone (John 14:6; Acts 4:12; Ephesians 2:8–9) and that human works play no part in salvation although they are generated by it (Ephesians 2:10). Salvation transforms a person's nature, giving him or her the ability and the desire to serve and obey God. The unresponsive heart of stone is changed into a sensitive heart of flesh that responds readily to God's voice (Ezekiel 36:25–27) and desires to glorify Him out of gratitude for the indescribable gift of salvation.

Reformed thought affirms that God works in history to redeem His chosen ones through a series of covenants. These covenants define His Law, assess penalties for breaking His Law, and provide for the imputation of Jesus' vicarious fulfillment of God's requirements to those God intends to redeem.[3]

The Reformed Faith affirms that we were created and exist solely to glorify God, and it denies that God exists to serve us. It affirms that God acts to glorify Himself by putting His attributes on display and that His self-glorifying actions are thoroughly righteous since He is the only Being in creation worthy of glorification. It denies that God is motivated to act *primarily* by man's needs; rather, it affirms that all of God's actions are motivated *primarily* for His own glory.

The Reformed Faith emerged as a distinct belief system during the sixteenth and seventeenth centuries when men like Luther, Calvin, Zwingli, and Knox fought against the Roman Catholic Church to restore Christian doctrine to biblical truth. These men were labeled *Reformers*, but they would have been better labeled *Restorers* since their goal was to correct abuses and distortions of Christianity that were rampant in the established Roman church. Reformed thinkers since their day have sought to align their own understanding of God and His actions in history as closely as possible to His revealed truth.

---

[1] This brief overview of basic Reformed beliefs is not intended to be a full explanation of or apologetic for the Reformed Faith. For a more detailed description and analysis of the Reformed Faith see: R. C. Sproul, *Grace Unknown* (Grand Rapids: Baker Books, 1997); Loraine Boettner, *The Reformed Faith* (Phillipsburg, N.J.: Presbyterian and Reformed, 1983); *Back to Basics: Rediscovering the Richness of the Reformed Faith*, ed. David G. Hagopian (Phillipsburg, N.J.: P & R Publishing, 1996); *The Westminster Confession of Faith* (with its accompanying Catechisms); or the theological writings of John Calvin, B. B. Warfield, Charles Hodge, and Louis Berkhof.

[2] Both of these truths are taught throughout the pages of Scripture; however, the sovereignty of God can be seen very clearly in Isaiah 40–60 and in Job 38–42, while the total depravity of man is described quite graphically in Romans 3:10–18.

[3] An excellent discussion of these covenants is contained in Chapter 5 of R. C. Sproul, *Grace Unknown*.

# The Purpose of Deo Volente Publishing

*"And do not be conformed to this world,
but be transformed by the renewing of your mind,
that you may prove what is that good and
acceptable and perfect will of God"*
Romans 12:2 (NKJV)

Deo Volente Publishing exists to help make the exhortation of Romans 12:2 a living, daily reality in the believer's life.

**Our goal is:**
- to edify believers in Christ,
- to encourage non-conformity to the world's standards,
- to exhort believers to live radically transformed lives that reflect the knowledge, enjoyment and practice of what is good, acceptable, and perfect in God's sight.

**We will endeavor to meet our goal by publishing material that:**
- is consistently Reformed in theology,
- is intensely practical for a daily Christian walk,
- encourages holy living in every aspect of life through the reforming power of God's Word.

## DEO VOLENTE
## PUBLISHING
P.O. BOX 4847
LOS ALAMOS, NM   87544
**Phone: (505)672-1622**
**FAX: (505)672-1615**